Bristol Potters 1775–1906

BRISTOL POTTERS

1775-1906

R. K. HENRYWOOD

REDCLIFFE
Bristol

First published in 1992 by
Redcliffe Press Ltd
49 Park St, Bristol

ISBN 1 872971 76 8

British Library Cataloguing-in-Publication Data.
A catalogue record for this book is available
from the British Library.

Typeset by Mayhew Typesetting,
Rhayader, Powys
Printed by WBC Print Ltd, Bridgend

Contents

Acknowledgements

The production of any book of this nature would be impossible without help and encouragement from many people. I would like to record my thanks to the librarians and staff of the public reference libraries at Barnstaple, Bath, Bridgwater, Bristol, Cardiff, Cheltenham, Exeter, Gloucester, Hereford, Manchester, Newport, Oxford, Plymouth, Salisbury, Taunton, Trowbridge and Worcester. Many other libraries and museums have also provided help and assistance, including the Bodleian Library at Oxford, Chetham's Library at Manchester, the Guildhall Library in London, the Institute of Historical Research of the University of London, the Manx Museum at Douglas on the Isle of Man, the West Country Studies Library at Exeter, and the William Salt Library at Stafford.

The illustrations are credited in the captions and most appear by kind permission of the Bristol Reference Library (BRL), the City of Bristol Record Office (BRO), the City of Bristol Museum and Art Gallery (BMAG), and the Somerset Local History Library at Taunton (TLH).

I would also like to express my personal thanks to Robert J. Harrison, Julian Lea-Jones, Tim R.N. Price and John S. Williams. I am particularly indebted to Karin Walton, Keeper of Applied Art at the City of Bristol Museum and Art Gallery, and to David Bromwich, Librarian of the Somerset Local History Library in Taunton.

Introduction

The manufacture of pottery in the Bristol area is known to date back to at least the thirteenth century although information about such early years is necessarily scarce. The manufacture of tin-glazed earthenware, or Bristol Delft, can be traced to the second half of the seventeenth century, and with many collectors interested in them, these wares have been documented in significant detail. Bristol was also noted for its early involvement with the manufacture of porcelain, and the two important eighteenth century factories have also been the subject of much research.

Following the demise of both the porcelain factories and the end of tin-glazed earthenware manufacture, the pottery industry in the city continued to develop, although the only establishment to receive much attention to date has been the Temple Back or Bristol Pottery. Contrary to common conception, it was by no means the only factory to exist. The city remained an important pottery centre throughout the nineteenth century and well into the twentieth, with large scale manufacture of redwares, and particularly stoneware. Indeed the Bristol stoneware, with its famous impervious glaze, was an important invention which was widely adopted elsewhere.

Apart from several books covering the eighteenth century Bristol porcelains, those interested in Bristol potters were served until recently by only two major works, Owen's *Two Centuries of Ceramic Art in Bristol* (1873) and Pountney's *Old Bristol Potteries* (1920), together with a chapter in Jewitt's *The Ceramic Art of Great Britain* (1878). Of these, Owen's work concentrated largely on the porcelain factories, and although Pountney covered both the tin-glazed earthenwares and the Bristol Pottery itself in significant detail, other nineteenth century wares were relegated to one short chapter of only thirty-four pages.

In more recent years interest in Bristol pottery has increased and there have been three notable additions to the literature. Frank Britton's *English Delftware in the Bristol Collection*, as its title implies, covers only the tin-glazed earthenwares made between about 1640 and 1780. It is a catalogue of examples in the Bristol Museum, and while it includes items made elsewhere, the strong local content is of great importance to those interested in Bristol pottery. Reg & Philomena Jackson's and Roger Price's monumental work *Bristol Potters and Potteries 1600–1800* is a major documentary study covering the seventeenth and eighteenth centuries. The third recent work, Sarah Levitt's *Pountney's — The Bristol Pottery at Fishponds 1905–1969*, is a fascinating social document which concentrates on the twentieth century, although it is largely anecdotal in content and thus of limited use to collectors.

Strangely enough, there has still been no major published history of the Bristol Pottery itself, despite the fact that its wares are relatively well-known and highly collectable. A useful short article by Cleo Witt entitled 'Good Cream Color Ware — The Bristol Pottery 1786–1968' appeared in *The Connoisseur* in 1979, timed to coincide with an exhibition of Bristol ceramics held at the City of Bristol Museum and Art Gallery in 1979 and early 1980. The accompanying exhibition catalogue, *Ceramics in Bristol — The Fine Wares 1670–1970*, is also an important document but unfortunately of limited use to collectors due to the relative lack of illustrations.

As many collectors will have found, these publications still leave a huge gap in that there is little coverage of the nineteenth century potters. It is tempting to feel that more general books on ceramics purporting to be comprehensive might provide some guidance but this is not the case. Apart from the specific works listed above, most collectors would have access to reference books of marks, but even these prove to be sadly deficient in their coverage of Bristol. For example, apart from the various proprietors of the Bristol Pottery, John Cushion's *Handbook of Pottery and Porcelain Marks* includes only six potters working in the period considered here, and even Geoffrey Godden's *Encyclopaedia of British Pottery and Porcelain Marks*, generally accepted to be the bible for collectors, lists only seven. It is this noted gap in the available literature that this survey is designed to fill.

Although an extensive and detailed documentary study similar to that undertaken by the Jacksons and Price for the earlier years would be of considerable historical interest, the immediate needs of collectors are felt to be best served by a more general survey. The approach employed here has been to investigate all Bristol potters listed in relevant local and national directories. While this approach may be criticised in an academic sense for being less than rigorous, it is a valuable exercise in its own right and is likely to answer many demands for additional information.

Contemporary directories were published to provide information of use in their day and as such they are a goldmine of information for the historian. Nevertheless, it is important to recognise that they are not entirely reliable. Mistakes were made in names, addresses, and even trades, and there were occasional omissions. In addition, the compilers were sometimes less than rigorous in their efforts, and some firms are listed for a brief time after their actual demise. However, in the specific case of Bristol, the number of directories is sufficiently large to make such errors reasonably obvious, and provided the problems are recognised and appropriate allowances are made there is no reason why the resulting information should not be of considerable use.

The present approach works particularly well for Bristol since the city was extensively covered, not only by local directories, including the unique annual series published by the Mathews family and their successors, but also within many county directories covering either Somerset or Gloucestershire, and in national directories such as the important series published by James Pigot and Isaac Slater. The whole subject of directories is fascinating and while any evaluation would be inappropriate here, all the directories referred to have been listed in detail for historical reference in the Appendix.

The scope of this survey was originally intended to cover just the nineteenth century, but despite some overlap with Jacksons and Price a start date of 1775 was eventually adopted. This was the year when the first Bristol directory appeared, amongst the first to be produced outside London, and its inclusion here along with twelve others published before 1800 appears logical. At the other end of the timescale, 1900 would have been a rather arbitrary cut-off date, and 1906 has been adopted as being much more significant since it coincides both with the start of Pountney's production at Fishponds and with the amalgamation of the Price and Powell stoneware firms.

In order to complete this survey, some 212 directories were located and examined, including multiple editions in several cases, and more than 5,000 relevant entries were noted. It is inevitable that a small number of entries will have been missed, particularly in some of the lengthy alphabetical lists, but few if any significant omissions are likely to remain. As noted earlier, this approach is not entirely rigorous but it has certainly yielded a list of potters with addresses, working periods, and much other pertinent information which has not previously been available. The main objective of filling the gap in our knowledge of Bristol potters of the nineteenth century has certainly been achieved. It is to be hoped that publication of this work will be of benefit to collectors and researchers alike, and that it might stimulate others to extend this groundwork with a more comprehensive survey in due course.

Alphabetical List of Potters

All potters and pottery firms appearing in relevant directories are listed below in alphabetical order. Where firms continued with only minor name changes, particularly family firms operating under the same surname, the information has been kept in a single entry with the various styles listed in the heading, which is always followed by the address or addresses of the firm. Information about changes of style and address changes can be found in the descriptive text, and cross-references to related firms have been included where they may be considered helpful.

All firms described or classified as manufacturers are listed here. The distinction between a potter and a retailer was particularly imprecise in the earlier years, and even towards the end of the period some stoneware dealers were described as manufacturers. Where any misunderstanding might remain, an appropriate comment has been included in the text. The confusion is particularly notable in the case of the various Ring family firms, most of which were involved in some way with the pottery trade as manufacturers, dealers or tobacco pipe makers, so they have been retained here for clarity and completeness, even where their involvement was somewhat indirect, as lime burners for example.

The descriptive text for each potter or firm includes any relevant information extracted from the directories, including details of advertisements where they have been located. Any inconsistencies noted in the directories are specifically noted, particularly where they affect either the name of a firm or the address. Information about products is included wherever it is available. The descriptive text is followed by a list of the directories in which the firm appears. Each directory is abbreviated to a date and the publisher's name, full details being available if required in the Appendix. The classification, if any, under which the firm is listed follows each directory name. An entry in an alphabetical list is noted as NC, indicating not classified, but other classifications are indicated by the following abbreviations:

BM	Bottle Manufacturers
BrickM	Brick Makers
BSW	Brown & Stone Warehouse Potters
BWM	Brown Ware Manufacturer
CGEn	China & Glass Enameller
ChinaE	China Enamellers
CMend	China Menders
ECM	Earthenware & China Manufacturers
ED	Earthenware Dealers
EM	Earthenware Manufacturers
GCED	Glass, China & Earthenware Dealers
GStain	Glass Stainers
NC	Not Classified
P	Potters
PB	Potters — Brown Ware
PS	Potters — Stone Ware
PSM	Potters & Stone Ware Manufacturers
SBJM	Stone Bottle & Jar Manufacturers
SD	Stoneware Dealers
SJBM	Stone Jar & Bottle Manufacturers
SJM	Stone Jar Manufacturers
SM	Stoneware Manufacturers
SMD	Stoneware Manufacturers & Dealers
SW	Stone Warehouses
TPM	Tobacco Pipe Makers

Albert Pottery Co.
St Philip's Marsh

The Albert Pottery Co. succeeded either Lavinia Cole (qv) or Joseph Hands (qv), both of whom are recorded at the pottery in the early 1870s. The company is listed in the Wright directories between 1875 and 1879, and also from 1886 onwards. There is no apparent reason for the break between 1879 and 1886, since the firm still appears in 1880 Slater, 1883 Kelly and 1885 Kelly. Except for the earlier Wright editions, all entries list the manager as John Moorse, given as John F. Moorse in the Town and County directories, although a few of the earlier directories quote his surname as Moore or Morse. He also has an individual entry, with his address given as the Albert Pottery, York Street, in 1906 Sharp.

The address of the Albert Pottery is usually listed simply as St Philip's Marsh, but the Kelly's directories list Albert Road in 1875, York Street between 1883 and 1894, and Victoria Terrace in 1897 and 1902. The only directory to mention the products is 1885 Kelly, which describes the firm as "makers of all kinds of flower and garden pots".

Directory entries:
Wright 1875–1878 NC, 1875–1879 P, 1886–1906 NC, 1886–1906 P

1875 Kelly P	1885 Kelly P	1897 Kelly P	1902 Kelly P
1876 Morris PSM	1889 Kelly P	1899 Town P	1902 Town P
1880 Slater EM	1891 Kelly P	1900 Town P	1903 Town P
1883 Kelly P	1894 Kelly P	1901 Town P	1906 Sharp P

Alsop, James
9 Water Lane (1775); Temple Street (1783–1803)

James Alsop is listed as a potter at 9 Water Lane in 1775 Sketchley, and as a brown stone potter at Temple Street in other directories between 1783 and 1803. The address is listed as 125 Temple Street in the Mathews directories from 1799.

Directory entries:
Mathews 1793–1803 NC

1775 Sketchley NC	1784 Bailey NC	1787 Bailey NC
1783 Bailey NC	1785 Browne NC	1792 Universal NC

Alsop, James jun.
Alsop, James, & Co.
Thomas Street

James Alsop junior is listed as a brown stone potter at Thomas Street in the Mathews directories of 1803 and 1805, and simply as a potter in 1805 Holden. The firm is listed in 1806 Mathews as James Alsop & Co.

Directory entries:
Mathews 1803–1806 NC
1805 Holden NC

Alsop, Uriah
Lawrence Hill

Uriah Alsop is listed as a potter at Lawrence Hill in the Mathews directories between 1809 and 1812.

Directory entries:
Mathews 1809–1812 NC

Amatt, Anthony
Thomas Street

Anthony Amatt does not appear as a potter in the directories although his activities are described in some detail by Pountney. He is listed as an individual with no trade given in Thomas Street in the Mathews directories between 1801 and 1818. The address is given as 56 Thomas Street in the 1818 edition only. He appears just once more in 1828 with his address listed as the King's Arms Tavern in Narrow Wine Street. His business was originally as a worsted manufacturer and his firm is listed as Amatt, Harris & Co., also in Thomas Street, between 1803 and 1817.

Pountney states that Amatt ran an iron-stone ware pottery at Crew's Hole in 1813, and went on to work as a manager at Powell's stoneware pottery when his worsted business finished about 1819. A fascinating notebook which Amatt used to record recipes and a few other notes survives and is now in the Bristol Reference Library. The Crew's Hole venture does not feature in the directories, and although Pountney describes an invoice heading in the notebook, he omitted to mention that it is hand-written, and hence possibly only a draft. Pountney's date of 1813 appears to be derived from other entries in the notebook; the invoice is neither dated nor bound into the book.

Directory entries:
Mathews 1801–1818 NC, 1828 NC

Andrews, E. & W.
Andrews & Lucas
Andrews & Sons
Thames Wharf, Temple Back

E. & W. Andrews appear in the classifications for both potters and stoneware manufacturers and dealers in the Wright directories between 1870 and 1877, but they were actually merchants and dealers rather than manufacturers. They succeeded Samuel Andrews (1847–1860) and they first appear in the Mathews directory of 1861 where they are described as "dealers in Stourbridge fire bricks, burrs, Bangor slates, Roman cement, Portland cement, scouring bricks, etc." By 1865 their entry is particularly detailed — "importers of Stourbridge and Flintshire fire bricks, burrs, squares, clay, &c.; stores for Roman and Portland cement, scouring bricks, agricultural and stone ware pipes, closet pans, and traps, urinals, roofing tiles, plaster of Paris, terra cotta, and common chimney pots, colors, &c." Their address is listed as 2 Temple Backs in 1877.

E. & W. Andrews were in turn succeeded by Andrews & Lucas who continued the business from 1878 to 1883, and then by Andrews & Sons. The last entry as stoneware manufacturers and dealers appeared under this name in 1893 although they continued to be listed as potters until 1904. From 1894 the style generally became W.J. Andrews & Sons, and there was another change to Herbert S. Andrews in 1904.

Directory entries:
Mathews 1861–1869 NC
Wright 1870–1906 NC, 1870–1904 P, 1870 SD, 1871–1893 SMD
1869 Bristol NC 1878 Owen SM 1904 Sharp SMD 1906 Sharp SMD

Appleford, Edward
27 Tower Street, Temple

Edward Appleford is listed as a potter at 27 Tower Street in the Wright directories between 1870 and 1873.

Directory entries:
Wright 1870–1872 NC, 1871–1873 P

Ashton, Green, Mathews & Co.
Temple Gate (1890–1893); 37 Victoria Street and Cathay (1894–1896)

Ashton, Green, Mathews & Co. are classified as stoneware manufacturers and dealers in the Wright directories between 1890 and 1893, but the alphabetical entries indicate that they were merchants and not manufacturers. They succeeded Ashton & Green Ltd. in 1890 and traded until 1896, specialising in bricks, slates, tiles, cement, and sanitary goods. The classified entries cease after 1893, and this corresponds with their move to Victoria Street with works at Cathay. The firm placed a series of advertisements in the Wright directories between 1890 and 1896.

Directory entries:
Wright 1890–1896 NC, 1890–1893 SMD

BRISTOL DIRECTORY ADVERTISING SHEET, 1895.

PLEASE NOTE ALTERATION OF ADDRESS.

ASHTON, GREEN, MATHEWS & Co.,
SLATE, TILE, CEMENT,
PLASTER, AND SANITARY GOODS MERCHANTS,
SLATERS AND TILERS,
37, VICTORIA STREET, BRISTOL,
(Near BRISTOL BRIDGE.)
Manufacture all the undermentioned Goods on their premises,—
SLATE
CISTERNS AND SINKS, PICKLING TANKS, LAVATORIES, URINALS, STEPS AND LANDINGS, BREWERY WORK OF ALL KINDS, GREENHOUSE AND DAIRY SHELVING, WINE BINS, CRESTING, HEARTH SLABS, DAMP COURSE, &c.

A Large Stock of the following Goods always on hand:—
Roofing Slates of all kinds. Bridgwater Roofing Tiles. Staffordshire Roofing Tiles. Staffordshire Paving Tiles and Bricks. Ridge Tiles and Finials. Glazed Stoneware Sinks. Sanitary Goods. Slate Slabs. Cement. Plaster. Laths. Hair, &c., &c.

PLEASE NOTE ALTERATION OF ADDRESS.
ENTIRELY DISTINCT FROM ASHTON & GREEN IRON CO.

Ashton, Green, Mathews & Co. *A typical advertisement from Wright's directory of 1895. An almost identically worded version appeared in 1891 quoting their earlier address as Temple Gate. (BRL)*

Austin, Pauline, & Co.
Boyce's Avenue, Clifton

Pauline Austin & Co. are classified as earthenware manufacturers in 1888 Bennett but as earthenware dealers in 1889 Bennett. Reference to the Wright directories indicates that Austin was only a dealer, operating a "Swiss and terra cotta depôt" at Boyce's Avenue, trading alone from 1879 and as Pauline Austin & Co. from 1885 until 1904. Two other addresses are listed from 1887; Park Street (until 1903) and 17 Triangle.

Directory entries:
Wright 1879–1904 NC
1888 Bennett EM 1889 Bennett ED

B

Baker, John
Baker, John & William
Baker, William & John
St Philip's Marsh

William & John Baker are listed as earthenware manufacturers at St Philip's Marsh and Canon's Marsh in 1858 Slater, whereas John & William Baker are listed as stoneware manufacturers at St Philip's Marsh in 1867 Morris, where they are described as "stoneware, drain-pipe, and firebrick manufacturers". Neither partnership is listed in the Mathews directories, although John Baker does appear as a drain pipe manufacturer at St Philip's Marsh, with his residence at 11 Newfoundland Street, between 1858 and 1867. William Baker was a builder and contractor at Canon's Marsh during this period.

Directory entries:
Mathews 1858–1867 NC
1858 Slater EM 1867 Morris SM

Beech, John
37 Welsh Back

John Beech is listed as a potter at 37 Welsh Back in 1775 Sketchley.

Directory entries:
1775 Sketchley NC

Brice & Reed
Temple Street

Brice & Reed are listed as brown stone potters at Temple Street in the Mathews directories of 1799 and 1801. It is probable that these entries are misprints for Price & Read (qv), although a family named Brice was active in manufacturing bricks at this period (see, for example, Hutchins & Brice and Hutchins, Brice & Co.).

Directory entries:
Mathews 1799–1801 NC

Bright, John
Bright, J. & J.
Bright, Joseph
Bright, Jane & Ann
Bright, Jane, & Co.
131 Temple Street

John Bright succeeded Hope & Bright (qv) at 131 Temple Street and is listed in directories from 1824 to 1830. The firm continued until 1853 and according to the Mathews directories traded in turn as J. & J. Bright (1831–1840), Joseph Bright (1841–1849), Jane & Ann Bright (1850–1852), and finally Bright & Co. (1853). This final partnership is listed as Jane Bright & Co. in 1853 Scammell.

All the partnerships produced stoneware and patent water pipes, and the "improved" stoneware is first mentioned in 1848 Hunt. A residence at Brighton Cottage, Upper Montpelier, is listed for J. & J. Bright between 1834 and 1840. The address is given as 130 Temple Street in 1839 Robson, and as 134 Temple Street in the Mathews classified entries between 1839 and 1854, but this appears to be a printing error which was never corrected. There are also other inconsistencies after 1841, particularly the partnership names which are often out of date in the Mathews classified listings. All directory entries from 1851 describe the firm as "improved glazed stoneware, closet-pan, eject, and water pipe manufacturers".

Directory entries:
Mathews 1824–1853 NC, 1824–1854 PS

1824 Pigot P	1842 Pigot P	1850 Hunt PS	1853 Scammell PS
1830 Pigot P	1846 Slater P	1850 Slater EM	1853 Scammell NC
1839 Robson P	1848 Hunt PS	1852 Scammell PS	

Bristol Fire Clay Co. Ltd.
Blackswarth or Crew's Hole Road, St George's

The Bristol Fire Clay Co. Ltd. is classified under stoneware manufacturers and dealers in the Wright directories between 1881 and 1893. Their address is given as Blackswarth, St George's, with an office and depôt at St Philip's Bridge. They appear in the alphabetical lists from 1884 through to 1906 (and beyond), with the works address listed as Crew's Hole Road, St George's, and the office at either 15 Passage Street (1884–1904) or 6 & 7 Lower Castle Street (from 1905). The firm placed a series of advertisements in the Wright directories between 1880 and 1896.

Directory entries:
Wright 1884–1906 NC, 1881–1893 SMD

Bristol Victoria Pottery Co. Ltd.
See: Victoria Pottery Co. Ltd.

Bullock, Thomas
95 Thomas Street

Thomas Bullock is listed as an earthenware potter at 95 Thomas Street in the Mathews directories of 1832 and 1833.

Directory entries:
Mathews 1832–1833 NC, 1833 PB

THE BRISTOL FIRE CLAY Co., LIMITED,
BLACKSWARTH, ST. GEORGES, near BRISTOL.

MANUFACTURERS OF

GLAZED AND SANITARY PIPES,
BENDS, ELBOWS, JUNCTIONS, &c.

PLAIN AND ORNAMENTAL

CHIMNEY POTS,
Fire Bricks, Burrs, Squares and Boiler Blocks, White Facing Bricks, Flooring Tiles, Vitrified Paving Bricks, Fire Clay, Cement, &c.

BRISTOL DIRECTORY ADVERTISING SHEET, 1882. 53A

THE BRISTOL FIRE CLAY Co., Limited.

The Bristol Fire Clay Co. Ltd. *Two advertisements copied from the Wright directories of 1880 and 1882. The second of these appeared regularly until 1896. (BRL)*

Butcher & Brooks
Butcher & Harris
Butcher, William
Butcher, William, & Co.
14 Nelson Street (1852–1861); Rupert Street (from 1862)

Butcher & Brooks are listed at 14 Nelson Street in the Mathews directories and elsewhere between 1852 and 1859. There is no consistency in the second partners name, which is listed as either Brooks or Brookes. They were succeeded in 1860 by Butcher & Harris, who moved to Rupert Street, the new address being listed from 1862. Butcher & Harris were in turn succeeded at Rupert Street by William Butcher, listed alone from 1864 to 1898, and then by William Butcher & Co., listed from 1899 to at least 1906. The entry in 1904 Sharp mentions the trading name of W. Norgrove.

Several entries from 1858 onwards claim that the firms were established in 1850, and a wholesale warehouse at Bell Lane is listed between 1859 and 1861. William Butcher's residence is listed as 13 Somerset Street, Kingsdown in 1858, 48 Hampton Park in some entries between 1864 and 1891, and 36 Hampton Park between 1892 and 1898.

The Mathews directories classifiy all the various partnerships as potters, stoneware potters, or stoneware manufacturers and dealers, although the alphabetical listings show that they were actually factors (or dealers) and not manufacturers, a typical description being "glazed stone ware drain and water pipe factors, dealers in fire-clay goods, cements, plasters, flooring tiles, etc." although Butcher & Brooks are described also as brick makers and earthenware manufacturers in 1858 Slater.

Directory entries:

Mathews 1852–1869 NC, 1852–1869 PS

Wright 1870–1906 NC, 1870–1904 P, 1870 SD, 1871–1893 SMD

1856 Kelly P	1869 Bristol NC	1878 Owen SM
1858 Slater EM	1872 Morris PSM	1904 Sharp SMD
1868 Slater EM	1876 Morris PSM	1906 Sharp SMD

C

Cantle, Ann

Lawrence Hill

Ann Cantle is listed as a brown ware potter at Lawrence Hill only in 1819 Mathews.

Directory entries:

Mathews 1819 NC

Carter, Henry

Carter, Henry, & Co.

Carter & Pountney

Water Lane, Temple Backs

Henry Carter is listed as an individual at Water Lane, Temple Backs, in the Mathews directory of 1797 but the Bristol Pottery still appears under the partnership of Ring & Carter. He is listed in sole control in the Mathews directories from 1798 to 1803, and in 1805 Holden. Thereafter the business is listed in the name of Henry Carter & Co. until 1813, and then Carter & Pountney in 1814 and 1815. From 1816 the style became Pountney & Allies (qv).

The early entries continue to describe the business as the "only Queen's ware manufactory", but from 1805 as "manufacturers of printed, painted, enamelled, & cream-coloured earthenwares". Henry Carter & Co. are also listed as sugar, chimney, and garden pot manufacturers between 1805 and 1807, while other entries for Carter & Pountney list them at the "Pottery coal wharf" at Temple Back. Henry Carter's residence is listed as Bull Lane, Kingsdown (1803–1806), and then as 7 Unity Street, College Green (1807–1813).

A "retail warehouse for china, glass, earthenwares, &c." at 14 Bath Street is listed from 1798 to 1813, and other entries indicate that this establishment was closely connected with the Ring family, since it is also listed under Joseph Ring (junior) from 1808 to 1813, followed by his wife Sarah Ring (qv) from 1814 to 1817.

Directory entries:

Mathews 1797–1815 NC

1805 Holden NC	1809 Holden NC	1811 Holden NC

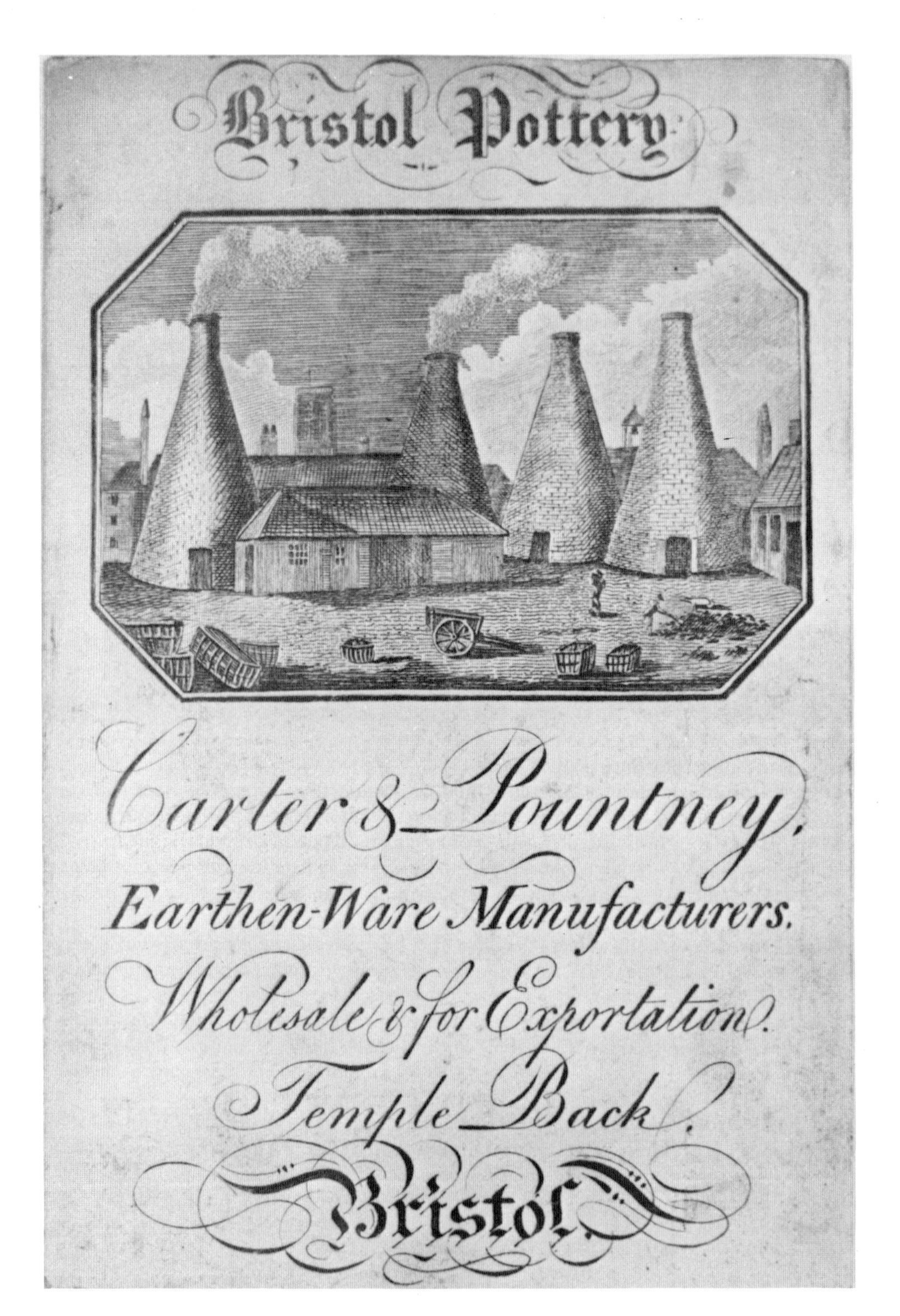
Bristol Pottery
Carter & Pountney,
Earthen-Ware Manufacturers.
Wholesale & for Exportation.
Temple Back.
Bristol.

Champion, Richard
Castle Green
Richard Champion is listed as a china manufacturer in 1775 Sketchley. The entry gives the address of his factory as 15 Castle Green and his house as number 17.
Directory entries:
1775 Sketchley NC

Chapman, Charlotte
Stokes Croft (until 1892); 11 Dighton Street, St James (from 1893)
Charlotte Chapman is classified as an earthenware dealer in 1889 Bennett, a list which includes several manufacturers. However, the Mathews directories confirm that she was only a dealer, succeeding Selina Chapman who is listed at 41 Stokes Croft between 1869 and 1871. Charlotte continued to trade from 41 Stokes Croft between 1872 and 1875, and then moved in turn to 81 Stokes Croft (1876–1892) and 11 Dighton Street, St James (1893–1895). The male side of the family traded as painters and decorators from the same addresses.
Directory entries:
Wright 1872–1895 NC
1889 Bennett ED

Church, Thomas
Various addresses
Thomas Church is listed as a crucible maker and earthenware manufacturer at Queen Ann Street, Barton Hill, in 1858 Slater and 1868 Slater. Alphabetical entries in the Mathews and Wright directories mention only crucible manufacture, although several different addresses are listed; Sussex Street, Dings (1850–1853 and also 1858 Slater), the George & Dragon, Temple Street (1852–1854), Bread Street, St Philip's (1854–1857), and Queen Ann Street, Barton Hill (1865–1874). There are no entries in the Mathews directories between 1858 and 1864, but an advertisement appears in 1861 Kelly giving his address as Barton Hill, St Philip's, and offering "a large stock of crucibles of all sizes for brass and iron founders" and "all kinds of best fire goods made to pattern". It also claims that he was established in 1840. His residence is given as Moorfields in 1855 and 26 Old Market Street in 1856 and 1857. He is listed as T. Church junior in 1869 Bristol, although no trade is mentioned.
Directory entries:
Mathews 1850–1857 NC, 1865–1869 NC
Wright 1870–1874 NC
1858 Slater EM   1868 Slater EM   1869 Bristol NC

Cole, Francis
Cole, Thomas
Cole, Lavinia
St Philip's Marsh
Francis Cole succeeded John Cole (see below) at St Philip's Marsh and is listed in the Mathews directories and elsewhere between 1836 and 1856, although some entries

Carter & Pountney. *A trade card featuring an engraving of the Bristol pottery. The same design had previously been used by Carter & Pountney and was later also copied by Pountney & Allies. (BMAG)*

remain in his name until 1862. He is described throughout as a brown stone and redware potter, with the addition of bricks and tiles between 1850 and 1853. He was succeeded by Thomas Cole who is listed between 1857 and 1868, with a single earlier entry in 1844 Mathews. Once again the products are described mainly as brown stone and redware with some mention of bricks and tiles, but with the addition of "improved highly-glazed stoneware" from 1858, and garden pots from 1865. Thomas Cole was in turn succeeded by Lavinia Cole who is listed between 1869 and 1873.

The factory name "Albert Pottery" first appears in 1869 Bristol, and the address is listed in full as the Albert Pottery, Albert Road, St Philip's Marsh in the Wright directories for 1872 and 1873. Directory entries from 1875 list the factory operating as the Albert Pottery Co. (qv).

Directory entries:

Mathews 1836–1869 NC, 1836–1855 PS, 1856–1869 PB
Wright 1870 NC, 1872–1873 NC, 1870–1873 P

1839 Robson P	1852 Scammell PS	1859 Harrison NC	1868 Slater EM
1842 Pigot P	1853 Scammell PS	1859 Harrison BSW	1869 Bristol NC
1846 Slater P	1856 Kelly P	1861 Kelly EM	
1850 Hunt PS	1857 Slater EM	1865 Webster EM	
1850 Slater EM	1858 Slater EM	1866 Harrod EM	

Cole, John

Great George Street Without (1820); St Philip's Marsh (from 1830)

Potters named John Cole are listed at Great George Street Without in 1820 Mathews, and at St Philip's Marsh in 1830 Pigot and in the Mathews directories between 1832 and 1835. It is not clear whether they are the same man. The first is described as a brown stone potter and the second as making brown stone and red ware.

Directory entries:

Mathews 1820 NC, 1820 PS, 1832–1835 NC, 1832–1835 PS
1830 Pigot P

Cole & Spokes

Avon Street, St Philip's

Cole & Spokes are listed only in two directories dating from 1815 and 1816. They are described simply as brown stone potters in 1815 Mathews, and may have been succeeded by Spokes & Bourne (qv).

Directory entries:

Mathews 1815 NC
1816 Evans P

Coles & Pearce

Avon Street, St Philip's

Coles & Pearce are listed as brown ware potters at Avon Street only in 1825 Mathews.

Directory entries:

Mathews 1825 NC, 1825 PB

ESTABLISHED 1840.

THOMAS CHURCH,
CRUCIBLE MANUFACTURER,
BARTON HILL, ST. PHILIP'S, BRISTOL.

T. CHURCH HAS ON HAND A LARGE STOCK OF CRUCIBLES OF ALL SIZES FOR BRASS AND IRON FOUNDERS.

ALL KINDS OF BEST FIRE GOODS MADE TO PATTERN.

Thomas Church. *A copy of an advertisement which appeared in Kelly's directory of 1861. (TLH)*

Colston & Pearse
Avon Street, St Philip's

Colston & Pearse are listed as potters at Avon Street, St Philip's, in 1815 Mathews and the three Evans directories of 1816–1818. The last two of these classify them as brown ware potters, and the second partner's name is given as Pearce in one entry in 1818. The first partner may have been connected with the John Colston who is listed by Mathews as having an earthenware shop at 15 West Street between 1806 and 1812.

Directory entries:
Mathews 1815 NC
1816 Evans P   1817 Evans PB   1818 Evans PB

Combes, Edward
See: Coombs, Edward

Cook, Charles
Cooke, Edward
Boot Lane, Bedminster

Charles Cook is listed as a brown ware potter at Boot Lane, Bedminster, in the Mathews directories between 1824 and 1847, although other directories describe him as making red ware. It is possible that he took over from Peter and Margaret Dean (qv) who worked at Boot Lane until 1823. The business was continued by Edward Cooke, probably related despite the change in surname, who is listed between 1848 and 1851.

Directory entries:
Mathews 1824–1847 NC, 1849 NC, 1824–1851 PB
1830 Pigot P   1839 Robson P   1842 Pigot P   1848 Hunt PS

Coombs, Edward
Coombs, Jane
Queen Street, St Philip's; St John's Bridge (1816–1818)

Edward Coombs is listed as a china mender at Queen Street in the Mathews directories of 1793 to 1805, at St John's Bridge in the Evans directories of 1816 to 1818,

and at Queen Street again in 1820 Mathews. The surname is given as Coombes in 1793 and Combes between 1795 and 1805. The entry in 1820 lists him as a "china and glass mender, &c.", and the same description was used for his widow, Jane Coombs, who is listed by Mathews from 1821 to 1823.
Directory entries:
Mathews 1793–1805 NC, 1820–1823 NC
1816 Evans CMend 1817 Evans CMend 1818 Evans CMend

Cooper & Co.
Avon Street, St Philip's

Cooper & Co. are classified as potters at Avon Street, St Philip's, in the Wright directories between 1888 and 1890, and also in 1889 Kelly. They are described as making red ware pottery.
Directory entries:
Wright 1889–1890 NC, 1888–1890 P
1889 Kelly P

Cottrell (Messrs.)
Cottrell, W.H. & T.B.
Lower Montague Street

Messrs. Cottrell are classified as stoneware manufacturers and dealers at Lower Montague Street in the Wright directories between 1882 and 1893. The alphabetical entries show that they ran a sanitary ware depôt there, and were not manufacturers. The business appears to have been an offshoot developed by William Cottrell, who was a ladder maker and ran a glass and china warehouse in Barrs Street. The style remained Messrs. Cottrell until 1894, but from 1895 the sanitary ware depôt appears in the names of W.H. & T.B. Cottrell, who continued the business until at least 1906. Interestingly enough, an early advertisement for the sanitary ware depôt in the 1885 Wright directory also appears in the name of W.H. & T.B. Cottrell.
Directory entries:
Wright 1882–1906 NC, 1882–1893 SMD
1904 Sharp SMD 1906 Sharp SMD

COTTRELL'S
FURNISHING
Cut Glass and China
SHOW ROOMS,
21 & 22, BARRS ST., BRISTOL.
Wholesale and for Export.
Parties Furnishing and other buyers should inspect our Stock, Cheapest, Largest, and Best Selected in the West of England.

W. H. & T. B. COTTRELL'S
SANITARY WARE, SLATE,
Cement & Plaster Depot.
MONTAGUE STREET,
St. James' Barton, BRISTOL.
All kinds of Bricks, Tiles, Slates, Chimney Pots, Drain Pipes, Bends, Junctions, Syphons, Ejects, S. & P. Traps, Gulleys, Kitchen Sinks, Closet Pans, Sewer Gas Traps, Staffordshire Blue Bricks, Garden Edging, Pennant Stone Paving, Firebricks, Burrs, Fireclay, Cement, Whiting, etc., etc.
Minton's Encaustic and Enamelled Tiles for Furniture, and other Decorations in Stock.

W.H. & T.B. Cottrell. *An advertisement from Wright's Directory of 1885 printed alongside another for the same firm's glass and china shop at Barrs Street. (BRL)*

Cox, George
Avon Street, St Philip's (1823–1827); Horse Fair (1825)

George Cox is listed as a stoneware potter at Avon Street in the Mathews directories between 1823 and 1827. A second address at Horse Fair is also given but only in 1825. A classified entry for J. Cox which appears in 1823 Mathews is almost certainly a misprint for the same man.

Directory entries:
Mathews 1823–1827 NC, 1823–1827 PS
1824 Pigot P

Cox, J.
See: Cox, George

Cox, Thomas
5 Evans Road and 11 Lower Redland Road (until 1891); Various other addresses (from 1892)

Thomas Cox is listed as a stoneware manufacturer in 1883 Kelly, and as a stoneware manufacturer and dealer in the Wright directories between 1884 and 1891, and also in the Sharp directories of 1904 and 1906. He was actually a builders' merchant and house decorator, not a manufacturer, one description reading "builder & general contractor, painter, glazier, paperhanger, tiler, slater &c.; oil, color, glass, cement, plaster & sanitary depôt". He worked at 5 Evans Road and 11 Lower Redland Road until 1891, then moved to other addresses including Clifton Down Station, where he worked until at least 1906.

Thomas Cox placed several advertisements in the Wright directories. The first appeared in 1883, followed by one series dating between 1885 and 1893, and another from 1895 to at least 1906.

Directory entries:
Wright 1884–1891 NC, 1893–1906 NC, 1884–1891 SMD
1883 Kelly SM 1904 Sharp SMD 1906 Sharp SMD

Crinks, Samuel
St Philip's (1792–1797); Crew's Hole (1798)

Samuel Crinks is first listed as a pot-maker at John Street, St Philip's, in 1792 Universal. He is also listed in the Mathews directories as a pot-maker and mason for glass works, initially at St Philip's between 1793 and 1797, and then at Crew's Hole in 1798.

Directory entries:
Mathews 1793–1798 NC
1792 Universal NC

Cripps, Richard
Cripps, Richard, & Son
Redcliff Wharf, Redcliff Back

Richard Cripps is classified as a potter in the Wright directories from 1871 to 1879 and Richard Cripps & Son are classified as stoneware manufacturers and dealers in 1877 and 1878. The alphabetical entries in the Mathews and Wright directories indicate that Cripps set up in business as a general wharfinger and warehouseman with agencies for cement and Doulton pipes in 1850, and the style Richard Cripps & Son is first listed in 1875.

Cripps acted as an agent and dealer and was not a manufacturer, being comprehensively described from 1860 as a "general wharfinger, warehouseman, superintendent of grain and other cargoes, marble merchant, agent for the best glazed stoneware pipes, chimney-pots, vases, &c., grindstones, cement, fire-bricks, burrs, &c.; haulier in general". His residence is listed as Grenville House, Redland, from 1873. The firm was succeeded by Gooddy, Cripps & Sons (qv), who are listed from 1879.

Directory entries:
Mathews 1850–1869 NC
Wright 1870–1878 NC, 1870–1879 P, 1877–1878 SMD
1861 Kelly SM   1869 Bristol NC

Crown Clay Co.

Crew's Hole (1880–1882); Ring's Wharf, Temple Back (1880–1886); Pipe Lane, Victoria Street (from 1887)

The Crown Clay Co. is classified under stoneware manufacturers and dealers in the Wright directories of 1887 and 1888. They were manufacturers of fire bricks, sanitary pipes, and terra cotta ware, and they first appear in the alphabetical lists in 1880 with works at Crew's Hole and a city depôt at Ring's Wharf, Temple Back. The firm was presumably sold to Andrew Knowles & Co. (qv), since they are listed as the proprietors from 1887, and the separate Crown Clay Co. listings cease after 1898. The firm placed a series of advertisements in the Wright directories between 1880 and 1888, followed by similar advertisements for Andrew Knowles & Co. from 1889 to 1902, and again in 1905.

Directory entries:
Wright 1880–1898 NC, 1887–1888 SMD

Crown Pottery Co.

St George's

The Crown Pottery Co. of St George's is classified under potters in the Wright directories between 1888 and 1904, and succeeded Arthur Ellis (qv) who operated the pottery until 1887. There was also some earlier connection with John Ellis who is listed as an earthenware manufacturer at the Crown Pottery in 1872 Morris and 1880 Slater. Presumably the accountant Alfred Hiley had some involvement with the firm, since he is classified as a potter and listed as an earthenware manufacturer at the pottery in 1889 Kelly and as an accountant with his residence at the pottery in the Wright directories between 1888 and 1890. No details of the pottery's products appear in any of the directories examined.

Directory entries:
Wright 1890–1904 NC, 1888–1904 P

1872 Morris PSM	1899 Town P	1901 Town P	1903 Town P
1880 Slater EM	1900 Town P	1902 Town P	

Curtis, John

81 Redcliff Street

John Curtis is first listed as an earthenware and glass man in 1783 Bailey, although subsequent directories make it clear that he was a china, glass and earthenware dealer and not a manufacturer. He traded from his "Staffordshire warehouse" in Redcliff

THOMAS COX

PAINTER, GLAZIER, PAPERHANGER,

AND CONTRACTOR FOR GENERAL HOUSE REPAIRS,

Oil, Colour, and Glass Stores, and Sanitary Depot,

10, LOWER REDLAND ROAD, BRISTOL.

THE REDLAND SANITARY WARE DEPÔT,

5, Evans' Road, and 11, Lower Redland Road,

(NEAR BLACKBOY HILL).

CEMENT, PLASTER, SLATES, TILES, SQUARES, CHIMNEY POTS, FIRE-CLAY GOODS, &c. OIL, COLOUR, & PAPER-HANGING WAREHOUSE.

THOS. COX, Proprietor.

THOS. COX, Builders' Merchant,

OIL, COLOR, AND GLASS STORES, &c.

11, LOWER REDLAND ROAD.

SANITARY WARE, BRICKS, TILES, SLATES, &c., &c.

CLIFTON DOWN STATION.

Telephone No. 1036.

THOMAS COX,

Telegrams "Cement, Bristol."

Coal, Brick, Slate, Tile, Cement, Plaster, and Sanitary Goods Merchant.

Head Offices—WHITELADIES GATE.

Cement & Sand Stores—8, THE GROVE (Queen Square).

Thomas Cox. *A selection of advertisements of the period. These appeared in 1883 Wright, 1889 Wright, 1890 Wright, and 1905 Wright respectively. (BRL and TLH)*

Street until 1805, after which he was succeeded by Cyples, Alloway & Co. The name is actually listed as Joseph Curtis in 1801 Mathews.

Directory entries:

Mathews 1793–1805 NC

1783 Bailey NC	1787 Bailey NC	1805 Holden NC
1785 Browne NC	1792 Universal NC	

Curtis, Joseph

See: Curtis, John

D

Daniel, Philip

Jacob Street (1793); David Street (1795–1798)

Philip Daniel is listed as a china mender in the early Mathews directories, which list his address as Jacob Street in 1793 and David Street between 1795 and 1798.

Directory entries:

Mathews 1793–1798

Davidson, Alfred, & Co.

46 Broad Quay

Alfred Davidson & Co. are classified as earthenware manufacturers in 1858 Slater, where they are listed as making stoneware at 46 Broad Quay. They do not appear in the Mathews directories of the period.

Directory entries:

1858 Slater EM

Dean, Peter

Dean, Margaret

Boot Lane, Bedminster

Peter Dean is listed as a potter at Boot Lane, Bedminster, in directories from 1792 through to 1812 and again from 1815 to 1821, although his surname is listed as Deane until 1803. He is described as a brown ware potter from 1815, and was succeeded by Margaret Dean, possibly his widow, who appears only in the Mathews directories of 1822 and 1823. It is possible that she was in turn succeeded by Charles Cook (qv) who is listed at Boot Lane from 1824.

Directory entries:

Mathews 1793–1812 NC, 1815–1822 NC, 1820–1821 PB, 1823 PB

1792 Universal NC	1811 Holden NC	1817 Evans PB
1809 Holden NC	1816 Evans P	1818 Evans PB

Deane, Abraham

12 Temple Street

Abraham Deane is listed as a potter at Temple Street in 1775 Sketchley.

Directory entries:

1775 Sketchley NC

Duffet, Josiah
Avon Street, St Philip's

Josiah Duffet is first listed as a potter at Avon Street in 1785 Browne, and appears in the Mathews directories from 1793 to 1809, and in 1811 Holden.

Directory entries:
Mathews 1793–1809 NC
1785 Browne NC   1792 Universal NC   1809 Holden NC   1811 Holden NC

Duffett, Henry
St Philip's Marsh; Lawrence Hill; Victoria Street, St Philip's

Henry Duffett is listed as proprietor of a brick and tile yard in the Mathews and Wright directories between 1836 and 1878. Addresses are listed as St Philip's Marsh (1836–1870), Lawrence Hill (1854–1878), and Victoria Street, St Philip's (1871–1876). Duffett's residence is listed as Barton Hill (1836–1838), 26 Centre Redcliff Crescent (1849–1865), 27 Centre Redcliff Crescent (1866–1876), and Oxford Terrace, Bishopston (1877 and 1878). It is not clear whether he was a manufacturer or only a dealer.

Directory entries:
Mathews 1836–1869 NC
Wright 1870–1878 NC
1869 Bristol NC

Duffett, James
Barton Hill (1810–1840); St Philip's Marsh (1828–1836)

James Duffett is listed as a redware potter at Barton Hill in the Mathews directories and elsewhere between 1810 and 1840, although the surname is listed as Duffet until about 1817. A second business as a brick and tile maker at St Philip's Marsh is listed between 1828 and 1836. There is also a note that Duffett succeeded J. Gibbs from 1828, although the meaning of this statement is not clear since the Hutchins partnerships in which Gibbs was involved appear to have continued until about 1836 (see Hutchins & Gibbs).

Directory entries:
Mathews 1810–1838 NC, 1820–1821 PB, 1823–1840 PB
1816 Evans P   1818 Evans PB   1824 Pigot P
1817 Evans PB   1822 Pigot P   1830 Pigot P

Duffett, John
Wilder Street

John Duffett was the first of a family of potters working at Pipe Lane, Temple Back (see below), but there is also a single entry for a John Duffett, described as a manufacturer of water pipes and chimney and garden pots at Wilder Street, in the alphabetical list only in 1843 Mathews. It is not known whether the two firms were related.

Directory entries:
Mathews 1843 NC

474 BRISTOL DIRECTORY ADVERTISING SHEET, 1880.

THE

CROWN CLAY CO.

RING'S WHARF, TEMPLE BACK,

BRISTOL,

MANUFACTURERS OF SUPERIOR

Fire Bricks, Burrs, Squares, Boiler Seatings, Cupola Bricks,

AND

Fire Clay Cement.

BEST GLAZED SANITARY PIPES,

BENDS, ELBOWS, SINGLE & DOUBLE JUNCTIONS, SYPHONS, GULLIES, S. & P. TRAPS, EJECTS, KITCHEN SINKS, and CLOSET PANS.

BEST QUALITY CHIMNEY POTS,

Of Various Patterns, Plain and Ornamental

VASES, TRUSSES & FLUE LININGS.

BEST RED PRESSED FACING BRICKS,

FLOORING SQUARES, etc., etc.

Roman Tiles. Pantiles. Ridge Tiles. Crease.

Best Portland Cement. Plaster.

And a variety of other goods always in Stock.

Works, CREW'S HOLE, near BRISTOL.

The Crown Clay Co. *One of a series of advertisements which appeared in the Wright directories between 1880 and 1883. (BRL)*

Duffett, John
Duffett, S., & Sons
Duffett, S., & Son
Duffett, Charles

124 Temple Street (until 1820); Pipe Lane, Temple Back (from 1817)

John Duffett is first listed as a potter at Temple Street in 1805 Mathews and the address is given as number 124 Temple Street from 1806 to 1820 (although it is misprinted as number 125 in 1811 Holden). The surname is normally shown as Duffet until about 1817. A second address at Pipe Lane, noted as the pottery, appears in the Mathews directories from 1817 and the last mention of Temple Street is in 1820. The only address shown in 1818 Evans is Commercial Road, but this probably relates to Duffett's residence, listed in 1822 Mathews as Hope Cottage, Commercial Road.

John Duffett is listed until 1831 when he was succeeded by S. Duffett & Sons, listed only in 1832, although the plural style may be a misprint since they were immediately followed by S. Duffett & Son, listed from 1833 to 1842. They were in turn succeeded by Charles Duffett who appears as a red ware potter in the Mathews and other directories between 1842 and 1854. He was succeeded by William Hutchings (qv).

The Duffetts are described throughout simply as red ware potters although 1839 Robson notes that S. Duffett & Son were red ware potters ''and manufacturers of chimney and garden pots, water pipes, etc.'' Charles Duffett's residence is listed in 1848 Hunt as Hope Cottage, Temple Back, presumably passed down the family from John Duffett. Another entry in the name of John Duffett, possibly unrelated, appears in 1843 Mathews (see separate section above).

Directory entries:

Mathews 1805–1854 NC, 1820–1821 PB, 1823–1854 PB

1809 Holden NC	1818 Evans PB	1839 Robson P	1850 Hunt PS
1811 Holden NC	1822 Pigot P	1842 Pigot P	1850 Slater EM
1816 Evans P	1824 Pigot P	1846 Slater P	1852 Scammell PS
1817 Evans PB	1830 Pigot P	1848 Hunt PS	1853 Scammell PS

BRISTOL DIRECTORY ADVERTISING SHEET, 1885. 15A

THE CROWN CLAY CO.,
RING'S WHARF, TEMPLE BACK, BRISTOL,
(Near the Great Western Railway Goods Station.)

BEST GLAZED SANITARY PIPES,
Bends, Junctions, Syphons, Gullies, Ejects, and Kitchen Sinks.

Chimney Pots, various patterns, Vases, Trusses, Flue Linings,
AND GARDEN EDGING TILES.

The "WASH OUT" and other patterns Closet Pans,
LAVATORY BASINS AND URINALS.
Stourbridge and Local Fire Bricks, Squares, Fire Clay, &c.,
BRICKS AND FLOORING TILES, RED, BUFF AND BLUE.
STABLE BRICKS AND GUTTERS, DIAMOND PAVINGS, ROMAN AND OTHER ROOFING TILES, RIDGES,
BEST LONDON PORTLAND CEMENT, PLASTER, WHITING,
AND A VARIETY OF OTHER GOODS.

The Crown Clay Co. *One of another series of advertisements which appeared in the Wright directories from 1884 through to 1888. (BRL)*

E

Eaves, John
Under the Bank
John Eaves was not a potter but is listed as a china enameller in the Mathews directories of 1807 and 1808 and in 1809 Holden. He may have been succeeded by Thomas Pardoe (qv), also a china enameller, who is listed at the same address from 1809.
Directory entries:
Mathews 1807–1808 NC
1809 Holden NC

Elbury, R.
Avon Street, St Philip's
Elbury is listed as a stoneware potter in 1844 Mathews, where he is described as a "red ware chimney & garden pot manufacturer".
Directory entries:
Mathews 1844 NC, 1844 PS

Ellis, Arthur
Crown Pottery, St George's
Arthur Ellis is listed as an earthenware manufacturer at the Crown Pottery, St George's, in 1885 Kelly and classified as a potter in the Wright directories between 1885 and 1887. Thereafter the pottery is listed as the Crown Pottery Co. (qv). Ellis does not appear in Wright's alphabetical lists, but he could be the Arthur Ellis who is listed with a china and glass warehouse at Batch between 1881 and 1885.
Directory entries:
Wright 1881–1885 NC, 1885–1887 P
1885 Kelly EM

Ellis, John, & Co.
Ellis, John
Ellis, Hawley & Co.
Ellis & Co. Ltd.
Thomas Street (1848–1849); Rich's Buildings, Redcross Street (1853–1870); Barton Hill (1856); Victoria Pottery, St Philip's Marsh (1865–1867); Crown Pottery, St George's (1872–1880)
John Ellis & Co. are first listed as stone and red ware potters in 1848 Hunt and as earthenware manufacturers in 1849 Mathews, both entries giving the address as 57 Thomas Street. There are no further entries until 1853 when John Ellis is listed alone at Rich's Buildings, Redcross Street, presumably succeeding William White (qv). Entries continue at the Redcross Street address only until 1864 in the Mathews directories, but as late as 1870 in the other directories.
There is a single reference to a partnership called Ellis, Hawley & Co. in 1856 Mathews, and the style John Ellis & Co. reappears only in 1859 Harrison where a second address at Bath Street is also listed. A further address at Barton Hill appears in 1856 Kelly. In 1865 he is listed in the Mathews directories at the Victoria Pottery, St Philip's Marsh, and from 1866 to 1869 entries refer to the Bristol Victoria Pottery

Co. Ltd. (qv). The style at the Victoria Pottery is listed as Ellis & Co. Ltd. in 1866 Kelly and 1867 Morris. His private residence is given as Conham Hall in 1868 and 1869. Ellis must also have had some connection with the St George's based Crown Pottery Co. (qv), since he is listed as an earthenware manufacturer there in 1872 Morris and 1880 Slater.

Ellis is initially described as a manufacturer of "Egyptian black and Rockingham tea pot, stone jug and ware", and from 1861 as a "manufacturer of stone and earthenware" and "wholesale dealer in British and foreign china and glass". Blue and white ware is mentioned specifically in 1865 Webster and 1866 Harrod.

Directory entries:
Mathews 1849 NC, 1849 P, 1853–1869 NC, 1853–1855 PS, 1856 P

1848 Hunt PS	1859 Harrison EM	1866 Harrod EM	1869 Bristol NC
1853 Scammell PS	1861 Kelly EM	1866 Kelly EM	1870 Kelly EM
1856 Kelly P	1863 Kelly EM	1866 Kelly P	1872 Morris PSM
1859 Harrison BSW	1865 Webster EM	1867 Morris P	1880 Slater EM

Encell, John
Encell, Mary
22 Bristol Back (1775–1797); 16 Old Market (1799)

John Encell is listed at 22 Bristol Back in 1775 Sketchley, described as a "glass maker, china and earthenware". This could indicate that he was a potter, but subsequent directories listing him at 16 Old Market in 1799 and Mary Encell at Bristol Back between 1785 and 1797 show that that they were dealers with a glass and Staffordshire warehouse. The surname varies, listed sometimes as Ensell or even Enscell.

Directory entries:
Mathews 1793–1799 NC

1775 Sketchley NC	1785 Browne NC	1787 Bailey NC	1792 Universal NC

Evans, John
5 Lewis's Buildings (1775); Brick Street (1785)

John Evans is listed as a potter at 5 Lewis's Buildings in 1775 Sketchley and as a brick maker at Brick Street in 1785 Browne.

Directory entries:

1775 Sketchley NC	1785 Browne NC

F

Fifield, William
William Fifield and his son, also William, are rightly celebrated as flower painters on Bristol pottery during the period 1810–55, but they are not listed in the Mathews directories of the period. They were never manufacturers. Examples of their decorating work are described by Pountney and several, including signed pieces, were included in the exhibition of 1979–80.

Fletcher, Thomas
131 Temple Street
Thomas Fletcher is listed at 131 Temple Street as a potter ''and earthen warehouse'' in 1775 Sketchley.
Directory entries:
1775 Sketchley NC

Flood & Hicks
Flood, Jonathan
Flood, Jonathan, & Co.
Flood & Co.
Temple Back; Avon Street, St Philip's (from 1829)
Jonathan Flood is listed as a red ware potter at Temple Back, near the Bristol Pottery, in the Mathews directories from 1818 through to 1847. In 1818 he was resident in Pipe Lane, and the entry in the Evans directory of that year lists Flood & Hicks as brown ware potters at Commercial Road (also Temple Back). The firm is listed as Jonathan Flood & Co. between 1822 and 1826, and simply as Flood & Co. in the Pigot directories of 1822 and 1824. From 1829 Flood took over the brick and tile works at Avon Street, St Philip's, previously operated by Samuel and Mary Sheppard (qv). The manufacture of water pipes is mentioned in the directories from 1837. The address is listed as Commercial Road, Temple Back, in 1846 Slater.
Directory entries:
Mathews 1818–1847 NC, 1820–1821 PB, 1823–1847 PB

1818 Evans PB	1824 Pigot P	1842 Pigot P
1822 Pigot P	1830 Pigot P	1846 Slater P

Flower, Joseph
The Quay; Corn Street
Joseph Flower is listed as a potter at number 2 the Key (sic) in 1775 Sketchley, and as a potter and earthenware man, presumably meaning a dealer, at Corn Street in 1785 Browne.
Directory entries:
1775 Sketchley NC   1785 Browne NC

Frank, Richard
Frank, Richard, & Co.
Temple Street
Richard Frank & Co. are listed as potters at Temple Street in three directories between 1783 and 1789, and Richard Franks (sic) is listed alone at Water Lane, Temple Street, in 1785 Browne.
Directory entries:
1783 Bailey NC   1784 Bailey NC   1785 Browne NC   1789 Tunnicliff NC

G

Gadd, Joseph, & Co.

Counter Slip (1787–1798); Temple Back (1792)

Joseph Gadd & Co. succeeded Patience & Gadd (qv) and are first listed as potters at Counter Slip in 1787 Bailey. They also appear at Counter Slip as brown stone potters in the Mathews directories between 1793 and 1798, although in 1792 Universal their address is given as Temple Back.

Directory entries:

Mathews 1793–1798 NC

1787 Bailey NC   1792 Universal NC

Galbraith, William

Nova Scotia Wharf (1884–1888); Poole's Wharf, Hotwell Road (from 1889)

William Galbraith is classified as a stoneware manufacturer and dealer in the Wright directories between 1884 and 1893, but the alphabetical entries show that he was a contractor, stone and coal merchant, and not a potter. He traded from Nova Scotia Wharf between 1884 and 1888, and then from Poole's Wharf, Hotwell Road, until at least 1906. His residence is listed as 6 Vincent's Parade, Hotwell's, until 1901, then Elm Cottage, Clifton Vale.

Directory entries:

Wright 1884–1906 NC, 1884–1893 SMD

Gibbs, J.

There is a note under James Duffett (qv) in the Mathews directories between 1828 and 1830 that he succeeded J. Gibbs. Gibbs does not appear in the directories except as a partner in the Hutchins firms of brick makers. The firms may have had more than one factory, one of which was taken over by Duffett from Gibbs when he left the firm in about 1827.

Godfrey, James

19 Temple Street

James Godfrey is listed as a potter at 19 Temple Street in 1775 Sketchley.

Directory entries:

1775 Sketchley NC

Gooddy, Cripps & Sons

Gooddy, Cripps & Sons Ltd.

Redcliff Back (1879–1891); Canon's Marsh (1892–1900)

Gooddy, Cripps & Sons succeeded Richard Cripps & Son and are classified as potters in the Wright directories between 1880 and 1900, initially at Redcliff Back but at Canon's Marsh from 1892. They were dealers and not manufacturers, the alphabetical listings describing them as marble merchants and wharfingers. The firm is listed as a limited company from 1880, and they were in turn succeeded by Walton, Gooddy & Cripps (qv).

Directory entries:

Wright 1879–1900 NC, 1880–1900 P

1899 Town P

Greaves, William
Greaves, William, & Co.
Head of the Quay (1787); Small Street (1792–1819)
William Greaves is listed as a potter at the Head of the Quay in 1787 Bailey. It is not clear whether this is the same William Greaves who appears as an earthenware man at Small Street in 1792 Universal, and as a Spanish wool merchant trading either alone or as William Greaves & Co. in the Mathews directories from 1793 to 1819. His business includes a ''wholesale earthenware and glass warehouse'', listed between 1801 and 1814. The address varies, being given mostly as number 1 Small Street, but as number 10 in 1798 and number 17 in 1819. St Michael's Hill is also mentioned between 1801 and 1814, possibly Greaves' residence.
Directory entries:
Mathews 1793–1819 NC
1787 Bailey NC 1792 Universal NC 1805 Holden NC

H

Hands, L.
Hands, Joseph R.
Albert Pottery, Albert Road, St Philip's Marsh
Joseph Hands is classified as a potter at the Albert Pottery, St Philip's Marsh, in 1870 Kelly, 1871 Wright, 1872 Morris and 1874 Wright. The erratic entries in the Wright directories also list Mrs. L. Hands at the pottery in 1870. Joseph's second name is listed as Rowland in 1870 Kelly and Richard in 1872 Morris. Directory entries from 1875 list the factory operating as the Albert Pottery Co. (qv).
Directory entries:
Wright 1870–1871 NC, 1874 NC, 1871 P, 1874 P
1870 Kelly P 1872 Morris PSM

Haskins' Potteries
Station Road, Montpelier
Haskins' Potteries are classified as potters at Station Road, Montpelier, in the Wright directories between 1887 and 1889. The alphabetical listings show that they ran a sanitary goods depôt, and they would have been dealers, not manufacturers.
Directory entries:
Wright 1887–1889 NC, 1887–1889 P

Hassall, John, & Co.
Hassall & Co.
Hassall, John
Leek Lane; Merchant Street (1814–1825); Norfolk Street (1826–1833)
John Hassall & Co. are listed as brown stone potters or stoneware manufacturers in the Mathews directories from 1813 to 1834. The style is given simply as Hassall & Co. in the Evans directories of 1816 to 1818, and John Hassall alone in 1830 Pigot. The surname is often listed as Hassell. The firm operated at Leek Lane throughout the period, but other addresses include Merchant Street (given as number 12 in 1822 and 1824 Pigot) from 1814 to 1825, then Norfolk Street from 1826 to 1833. A further

address at 33 Thrissel Street appears in 1834 but this is probably Hassall's residence, since he is listed as an individual there in 1835 with no trade given.

Directory entries:

Mathews 1813–1835 NC, 1820–1821 PS, 1823–1834 PS

1816 Evans GCED	1818 Evans PS	1824 Pigot P
1817 Evans PS	1822 Pigot P	1830 Pigot P

Hawley, James George
Hawley, George Henry & James Alfred
Hawley & Son
Hawley & Co.
Hawley Brothers

Temple Back

J.G. Hawley is listed as an individual at 2 Water Lane, Temple, in the Mathews directories between 1851 and 1855 and at Cornwallis House, Stapleton Road, in 1857 and 1858. Thereafter he is described as a commercial traveller at various addresses, namely 3 Lawrence Place, New River (1860), 19 Centre Redcliff Crescent (1861–2), and Langton Street (1863). Between 1865 and 1868 he appears as a commercial traveller and agent at 3 Laura Place, New River, and he is listed again as just a commercial traveller at 18 Somerset Square in the Wright directories of 1870–3 and also in 1869 Bristol.

The addresses listed suggest that Hawley may originally have had some connection with the Bristol Pottery at Temple Back, and with the Cornwallis Pottery in Stapleton Road which traded for a short period c.1857–58 as Morgan & Hawley (qv). The name Hawley also occurs c.1856 in the short-lived Redcross Street partnership of Ellis, Hawley & Co. (qv).

Hawley is first listed as a potter in his own right in 1875 Kelly and 1875 Wright, described as a redware manufacturer at Temple Back. Similar entries continue until 1888 although stoneware is mentioned instead of redware from 1876 or 1877. His residence is listed as 18 Somerset Square throughout this period.

The factory is named as the Temple Stoneware Pottery in 1883 Kelly, where the date of establishment is claimed to be 1802 and the manufacture of the improved stoneware is mentioned. This directory also refers to Hawley & Son who were trading separately as tobacco pipe manufacturers, also at Temple Back, until about 1892, although this firm appears in the Wright directories only in 1891 and 1892.

J.G. Hawley was succeeded by G.H. & J.A. Hawley, listed between 1889 and 1892, and then by Hawley & Co., listed between 1893 and 1898, who appear to have absorbed the tobacco pipe business of Hawley & Son. They were in turn succeeded by Hawley Brothers, listed between 1899 and 1901. Hawley & Co. are still listed in 1902 Kelly, despite the fact that the firm appears to have ceased trading by this date. James Alfred Hawley was still living at 18 Somerset Square as late as 1897.

Directory entries:

Mathews 1851–55 NC, 1857–1858 NC, 1860–63 NC, 1865-68 NC

Wright 1870–73 NC, 1875–1901 NC, 1875 P, 1878–1901 P, 1876–1893 SMD

1869 Bristol NC	1879 Kelly SM	1885 Kelly SM	1897 Kelly P
1875 Kelly P	1880 Slater EM	1889 Kelly P	1899 Town P
1876 Morris PSM	1883 Kelly SM	1891 Kelly P	1900 Town P
1878 Owen SM	1885 Kelly NC	1894 Kelly P	1902 Kelly P

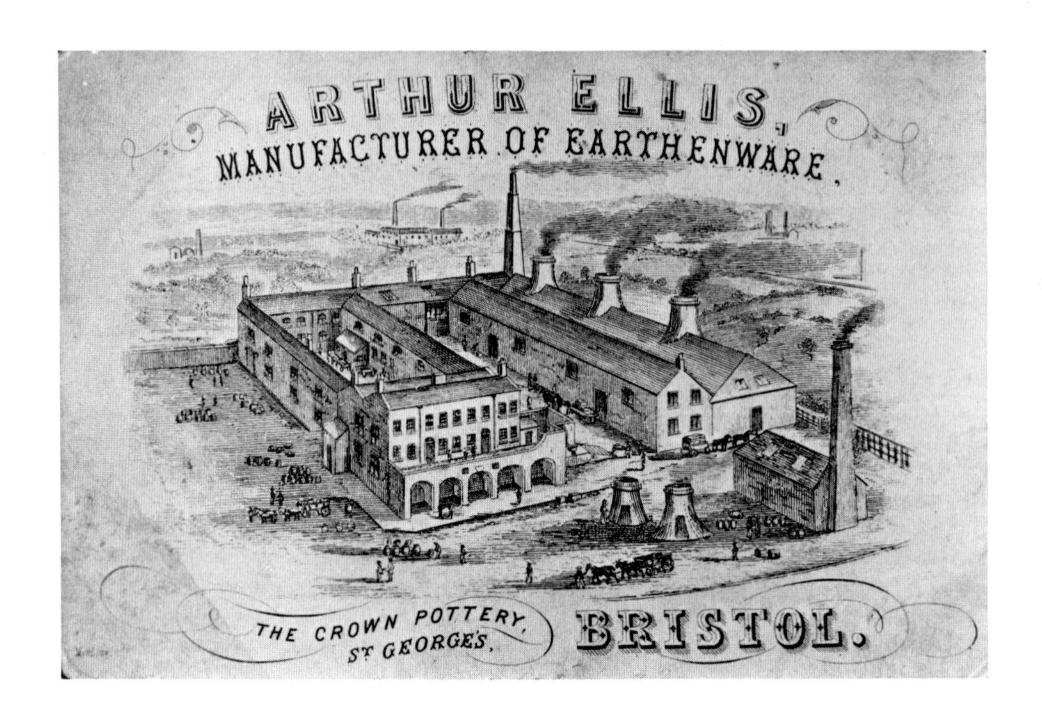

Arthur Ellis. *A rare surviving trade card, engraved by Mardons, showing the Crown Pottery at St. George's. (BMAG/Private collection)*

Heywood, William
Temple Backs

William Heywood is classified as a stoneware potter in 1852 Scammell, but he does not appear in the Mathews or other directories of the period.

Directory entries:
1852 Scammell PS

Hickery, Thomas
Hickery, Thomas, & Son
Hickery, Edwin C.
St Silas Pottery, St Philip's Marsh

Thomas Hickery & Son are classified as potters in the Wright directories from 1895 to 1899, but they first appear as potters and tile makers in the Kelly directories some ten years before. Thomas Hickery himself is listed as a brick and tile maker even earlier, in 1869 Bristol. The Wright directories also list William Hickery as a brick and tile maker from 1887 to at least 1906, but this was apparently a separate business. Thomas Hickery & Son were succeeded by Edwin C. Hickery, presumably the son, who continued the business at the St Silas Pottery from 1900 to 1903. There are few references to the products, only red ware being mentioned.

Directory entries:
Wright 1895–1903 NC, 1895–1903 P

1869 Bristol NC	1891 Kelly P	1902 Kelly P	1902 Town P
1885 Kelly P	1897 Kelly P	1900 Town P	1903 Town P
1889 Kelly P	1899 Town P	1901 Town P	

Hiley, Alfred
Crown Pottery, St George's

Alfred Hiley is classified as a potter and listed as an earthenware manufacturer at the Crown Pottery, St George, in 1889 Kelly, but the Wright directories of the period list him as an accountant in Corn Street, with his residence at the pottery between 1888 and 1890. Therafter he is listed only as a private individual at 97 Kingsdown Parade. Presumably his legal activities included some involvement with the pottery business.

Directory entries:
Wright 1887–1891 NC
1889 Kelly P

Hill, James
6 Guinea Street

James Hill is listed as an earthen-pot maker at 6 Guinea Street in 1775 Sketchley. He is still listed as living in Guinea Street in 1785 Browne and 1787 Bailey, although no trade is given in either case.

Directory entries:
1775 Sketchley NC 1785 Browne NC 1787 Bailey NC

Hill, Moses
4 Unity Street

Moses Hill is listed as a china maker at 4 Unity Street in 1775 Sketchley.

Directory entries:
1775 Sketchley NC

Hollister, Stephen
Barton Hill Pottery, Queen Ann Street, Barton Hill

Stephen Hollister is listed as a potter at the Barton Hill Pottery in 1887 Wright.

Directory entries:
Wright 1887 NC, 1887 P

Hope, John
Hope & Bright
Temple Street

John Hope is first listed as a stone potter in Temple Street in 1783 Bailey, and is described as a brown stone ware manufacturer in 1787 Bailey. He is listed in the Mathews directories from 1793 through to 1811, his address being noted as 131

Temple Street from 1805. Entries in 1792 Universal and the Mathews directories between 1797 and 1801 also list 8 Somerset Square, presumably his residence. His products are described as stoneware and patent water pipes from 1809. He was succeeded by the partnership Hope & Bright who continued to produce stoneware and the patent water pipes from 1812 until 1823. The entries in 1822 and 1823 refer to the original stoneware. Hope & Bright were in turn succeeded by John Bright (qv).

Directory entries:

Mathews 1793–1823 NC, 1820–1821 PS, 1823 PS

1783 Bailey NC	1787 Bailey NC	1811 Holden NC	1822 Pigot P
1784 Bailey NC	1792 Universal NC	1817 Evans PS	
1785 Browne NC	1809 Holden NC	1818 Evans PS	

Hornblower, John

Lower Castle Street

John Hornblower was not a potter, but is listed as a glass stainer and china enameller in the Mathews and Evans directories between 1817 and 1819. His address is given as 11 Lower Castle Street in 1817 Mathews, but as number 14 in all listings in 1818 and 1819. The reference to china enamelling is omitted from the 1819 Mathews entry, which reads simply "glass burner and stainer".

Directory entries:

Mathews 1817–1819 NC

1817 Evans GStain   1818 Evans NC

Hutchings, Walter, & Co.

See: Hutchings, William, & Co.

Hutchings, William
Hutchings, William, & Co.
Hutchings, William J. & G.S
Hutchings, William, & Son
Hutchings, W. & G.

Pipe Lane, Temple (1856–1906); Barton Hill (1856–1864); Temple Back (1861–1872); St Philip's Marsh (1862–1885)

William Hutchings succeeded Charles Duffett at Pipe Lane and is listed as a manufacturer of red ware, garden and chimney pots at both Pipe Lane and Barton Hill in the Mathews directories between 1856 and 1864. Thereafter the Barton Hill address no longer appears, but he is also listed as a brick and tile manufacturer at St Philip's Marsh from 1862. He took over the redware pottery at Temple Back which was previously run by Jonathan Flood and the Webb Family, and that factory is listed separately by Mathews between 1861 and 1872, the address appearing as 18 Temple Backs in 1871 and 1872. Otherwise Hutchings is listed alone in the Mathews directories until 1869, but as William Hutchings & Co. in the Wright directories from 1870 to 1874.

Other directories are somewhat confusing in this period, the style appearing almost randomly as William Hutchings or as William Hutchings & Co. Other styles to appear include Walter Hutchings & Co. in 1856 Kelly (presumably a misprint), William B. Hutchings & Co. in 1857 Slater, and William J. & G.S. Hutchings in 1859 Harrison. From 1875 the situation is somewhat clearer, with the Wright directories recording the firm in their alphabetical lists as William Hutchings & Son

(1875–1880), William Hutchings again (1881–1882), and finally William Hutchings & Co. again (1883 to at least 1906). The dates in the classified entries vary slightly and they also show a partnership of W. & G. Hutchings in 1883 and 1884. The St Philip's address does not appear after 1885, the only remaining address being Pipe Lane, listed as 46 Pipe Lane in 1897 Kelly, 1902 Kelly and 1904 Sharp, and often as Pipe Lane, Victoria Street, after 1879. One strange entry is in 1858 Slater where Hutchings is listed as a red earthenware manufacturer and gas fitter at 34 Host Street.

The entries almost always list the products as red ware, but sometimes they are described as brown ware, and there are frequent references to draining pipes, water pipes, and garden pots. The products at the Temple Back factory were similar, although at St Philip's Marsh they are generally listed only as bricks and tiles. The final entries at Pipe Lane list the firm as "manufacturers of all kinds of garden and fancy pots, and red ware". Hutchings' private residence is listed as 12 Somerset Square between 1857 and 1866, and as 13 Redcliff Parade West between 1867 and 1872. His surname is occasionally printed as Hutchins.

Directory entries:

Mathews 1856–1869 NC, 1855–1869 PB, 1861–1869 PS

Wright 1870–1877 NC, 1879–1906 NC, 1870–1874 P, 1880–1906 P, 1880–1893 SMD

1856 Kelly P	1866 Harrod EM	1879 Kelly P	1897 Kelly P
1857 Slater EM	1866 Kelly P	1880 Slater EM	1899 Town P
1858 Slater EM	1867 Morris P	1883 Kelly P	1900 Town P
1859 Harrison BSW	1868 Slater EM	1885 Kelly P	1901 Town P
1861 Kelly EM	1869 Bristol NC	1888 Bennett EM	1902 Kelly P
1861 Kelly P	1870 Kelly P	1889 Bennett ED	1902 Town P
1863 Kelly EM	1872 Morris PSM	1889 Kelly P	1903 Town P
1863 Kelly P	1875 Kelly P	1891 Kelly P	1904 Sharp P
1865 Webster EM	1876 Morris PSM	1894 Kelly P	1906 Sharp P

Hutchins, Brice & Co.
Hutchins, John
Hutchins & Brice
Hutchins, John & Edward
Hutchins, John, & Co.
Hutchins, Edward, Son & Co.
Hutchins & Gibbs
Hutchins, Edward, & Co.
Hutchins & Co.
Hutchins, Gibbs & Co.
St Philip's

A family named Hutchins was active in several partnerships making bricks at St Philip's between 1785 and 1836. The first entry is for Hutchins, Brice & Co. listed as brick makers and lime burners at Avon Street in 1785 Browne, and this partnership is listed in most directories until 1803, although the address is given as Cheese Lane in 1792 Universal. In 1797 Mathews there is also an entry for John Hutchins, listed as a brick maker, lime burner, starch maker and maltster. From 1805 the partnership is given as Hutchins & Brice who are listed in the Mathews directories as brick makers and lime burners until 1811.

Thereafter there were rapid changes in the firm (or firms); partnerships listed including John & Edward Hutchins (1812), John Hutchins & Co. (1812 and

1816–1818), Edward Hutchins, Son & Co. (1813), Hutchins & Gibbs (1814 and 1823–1827), Edward Hutchins & Co. (1815–1816), Hutchins & Co. (1819–1820 and 1828–1836), and Hutchins, Gibbs & Co. (1821–1822). All the partnerships are listed as brick makers but the lime burning business is not mentioned after 1813.

In the earlier years the address is shown as either Avon Street or Cheese Lane, but the last mention of Avon Street appears in 1814 when the address is described as "next door to the Full Moon". Thereafter only Cheese Lane is given. There is a note under James Duffett (qv) in the Mathews directories between 1828 and 1830 that he succeeded J. Gibbs. The meaning of this is not clear but perhaps the Hutchins partnerships had more than one factory, one of which was taken over by Duffett from Gibbs when he left the Hutchins firm in about 1827.

Directory entries:
Mathews 1793–1836 NC

1785 Browne NC	1792 Universal NC	1818 Evans Misc.
1787 Bailey NC	1816 Evans BrickM	

J

James, Philip
30 Ellbroad Street

An entry in 1775 Sketchley lists "James Phillips" as a china painter at 30 Ellbroad Street. The alphabetical order suggests that the surname is James, but the plural Phillips could raise some doubt. However, the confusion is resolved by Jackson and Price, who quote other sources giving his name as Philip James.

Directory entries:
1775 Sketchley NC

Jenkins, Henry
63 Quarrington Road, Horfield

Henry Jenkins is classified as a potter in the Wright directories of 1905 and 1906, but the alphabetical entries make it clear that he was mainly a greengrocer who traded also as a pottery merchant. The first name is misprinted as Herbert in the 1905 classification.

Directory entries:
Wright 1905–1907 NC, 1905–1906 P

Jenkins, Herbert
See: Jenkins, Henry

Johnson, John
16 Counter Slip

John Johnson is listed as a potter at 16 Counter Slip in 1775 Sketchley.

Directory entries:
1775 Sketchley NC

Jones, C.
Staple Hill
C. Jones is classified as an earthenware dealer in 1889 Bennett, a list which includes several manufacturers. However, no trader of this name appears in the Mathews directories of the period, and he or she was almost certainly only an earthenware dealer.
Directory entries:
1889 Bennett ED

K

Keeling, Thomas
Avon Street, St Philip's
Thomas Keeling is listed as a potter in the Mathews directories of 1801 and 1805, but not in 1803.
Directory entries:
Mathews 1801 NC, 1805 NC

Knowles, Andrew
Knowles, Andrew, & Co.
Pipe Lane, Temple; Various other addresses (from 1893)
Andrew Knowles is listed in the Wright directories as proprietor of the Crown Clay Co. in 1887 and 1888. The trading style became Andrew Knowles & Co. in 1889, and this continued until at least 1906, although the Crown Clay Co. name was dropped after 1898. The Pipe Lane address is described as a sanitary depôt from 1893 when a second address at Station Road, Montpelier, was added. Other addresses to be listed include Lawrence Hill (1897–1901), and an office at Ring's Wharf, Temple Back (from 1905). The trade in sanitary ware is listed as their main business in 1904 Sharp. The firm continued the series of advertisements in the Wright directories started by the Crown Clay Co. in 1880. They appear in the name of Andrew Knowles & Co. from 1889 to 1902, and again in 1905.
Directory entries:
Wright 1887–1906 NC, 1889–1893 SMD, 1891–1906 P
1904 Sharp SMD   1906 Sharp SMD

BRISTOL DIRECTORY ADVERTISING SHEET, 1894. 45A

ANDREW KNOWLES & CO.,

(THE CROWN CLAY CO.)

PIPE LANE, VICTORIA ST., BRISTOL.

(Opposite the Great Western Railway Goods Station.) *Telephone No. 372.*

BRANCH DEPOT: MONTPELIER STATION.

BEST GLAZED SANITARY PIPES,

Bends, Junctions, Syphons, Gullies, Ejects and Kitchen Sinks.

CHIMNEY POTS, VARIOUS PATTERNS, VASES, TRUSSES, FLUE LININGS, AND GARDEN EDGING TILES.

THE "WASH OUT" AND OTHER PATTERN CLOSET PANS.

LAVATORY BASINS AND URINALS.

Stourbridge and Local Fire Bricks, Squares, Fire Clay, &c

RED, BUFF AND BLUE BRICKS, AND FLOORING TILES.

STABLE BRICKS AND GUTTERS, DIAPER PAVINGS, ROMAN AND OTHER ROOFING TILES, RIDGES.

LONDON PORTLAND, AND PARIAN CEMENTS.

PLASTER, WHITING, HAIR, LATHS, SLATES, and a Variety of other Goods.

Andrew Knowles & Co.,

Pipe Lane, Victoria Street,

BRISTOL.

MANUFACTURERS OF

Sanitary Pipes, Kitchen Sinks, &c.,
Garden Tiles, Chimney Pots, Closet Pans & Urinals.
Fire Bricks, Burrs and Clay.
Red, Buff and Blue Bricks and Flooring Tiles, Stable Bricks, Pavings, Roofing Tiles and Ridges.

IMPORTERS OF

Best Portland Cement, Plaster, Whiting, Sand, Slates.

DEPÔTS AT

Montpelier Station & Redcliff Backs.

Telephones 372 & 1022. 26

Telegrams: "Knowles, Pipe Lane, Bristol."

Andrew Knowles & Co. *Two typical advertisements which appeared in Wright's directory of 1894 and Kelly's directory of 1902. Similar advertisements appeared from 1889. (BRL)*

M

Machem, William
See: Matchin, William

Matchin, William
Matchin, Edward
Matchin, Jane
Matchin, B. & E.
Matchin, B.
Matchin, R.
Matchin, Benjamin
Wilder Street

William Matchin is first listed as a potter at 15 & 18 Wilder Street in 1775 Sketchley. The next entry is in 1792 Universal (where the surname appears as Machem), and thereafter he is listed in the Mathews directories from 1793 to 1812, the address appearing as Wilder Street throughout but as number 9 in 1812. He is also listed as Clerk of St James's Church from 1793 to 1799, and as Clerk of Temple Parish Vicarage House in 1812. He was succeeded by Edward Matchin, who is listed in 1813 and 1814, and then by Jane Matchin, listed from 1815 to 1818. The alphabetical listings in the Mathews directories then show B. & E. Matchin (1819), B. Matchin (1820–1828), R. Matchin (1829–1832) and finally Benjamin Matchin (1834–1837). The classified entries vary slightly in dates, but one significant difference is that R. Matchin does not appear, the initial B. is still given from 1829 to 1832. Unfortunately this conflict is not resolved by other directories although Benjamin Matchin is listed in 1830 Pigot.

The address is given as 9 Wilder Street except in 1817 when it is shown as number 3 (presumably a misprint), and the surname is occasionally printed as Machin. The firm is decribed as ''wholesale stone, red and glazed ware, chimney and garden pot manufacturers'' in 1819 but subsequent descriptions are shorter, just ''red and glazed ware'' from 1825, and simply ''potter'' from 1834.

Directory entries:
Mathews 1793–1832 NC, 1834–1837 NC, 1820–1821 PB, 1823–1837 PB

1775 Sketchley NC	1811 Holden NC	1818 Evans PB	1830 Pigot P
1792 Universal NC	1816 Evans P	1822 Pigot P	
1809 Holden NC	1817 Evans PB	1824 Pigot P	

Maule, William, & Sons
Stapleton Road

William Maule & Sons are listed as horticultural potters at Stapleton Road in the Mathews and Wright directories between 1854 and 1884. According to the Mathews directories, the firm began as nurserymen, operating as William Maule & Co. at Lower Easton in 1815, the Stapleton road address dating from 1820. The surname appears occasionally as Maul in the earlier years, and from 1817 they were described as nurserymen, seedsmen and florists. A second address at Stoke Gifford is listed from 1836, and a third in Broadmead between 1837 and 1846. The style became William Maule & Sons in 1847. The manufacture of horticultural pottery began in

1854 and continued until 1884, when the firm reverted to their traditional nursery business. Their final appearance is in 1889 Mathews.

Directory entries:
Mathews 1847–1869 NC, 1854–1869 PB
Wright 1870–1889 NC, 1870–1884 P

1857 Slater EM	1863 Kelly P	1867 Morris P	1872 Morris PSM
1858 Slater EM	1865 Webster EM	1868 Slater EM	1876 Morris PSM
1859 Harrison BSW	1866 Harrod EM	1869 Bristol NC	
1861 Kelly P	1866 Kelly P	1870 Kelly P	

Mayer & Co.
Cornwallis Pottery, Stapleton Road

Mayer & Co. appear to have succeeded Morgan & Hawley (qv) at the Cornwallis Pottery, and are listed as earthenware manufacturers only in 1858 Slater.

Directory entries:
1858 Slater EM

Mayer, Boulton & Co.
Stapleton Road

Mayer, Boulton & Co. (the second name appears also as Boulten) are listed only in 1855 Mathews. The alphabetical listing describes them as porcelain and earthenware manufacturers, but they are classified as stoneware potters, and they made sanitary pipes at Nailsea where they are stated to have succeeded Coathupes & Co. A London depôt at wharf number 10 or 18 in the City Basin is also listed.

Directory entries:
Mathews 1855 NC, 1855 PS

Maynard, William
St Philip's (1783–1797); Counter Slip (1798–1801)

William Maynard is listed as a potter in most directories between 1783 and 1801. His address appears as Bread Street from 1787 to 1797, then Counter Slip. He is noted as William junior in the two Bailey directories of 1783 and 1784. He is described as a brown stone and red ware potter in 1787 Bailey, and by Mathews as either a potter and chimney mould maker (1793–1797), or a garden pot, glazed ware, chimney pot and water pipe manufacturer (1798–1801). His surname is listed phonetically as Mineard in 1792 Universal.

Directory entries:
Mathews 1793–1801 NC

1783 Bailey NC	1784 Bailey NC	1787 Bailey NC	1792 Universal NC

Melsom, Edward, & Co.
Melsom, Edward & Francis
Melsom, F. & E.
Melsom, Edward
Melsom, Francis
Avon Street, St Philip's (1830–1836); 124 Temple Street (from 1837)

Following the partnership of Milsom & Melsom (qv) which was last listed in 1826, the Melsom family set up in business at Avon Street, St Philip's. The first listing is in the name of Edward Melsom & Co. in 1830 Mathews, but this was immediately followed by Edward & Francis Melsom who are listed as stoneware potters and patent water pipe manufacturers from 1831 through to 1859. The address is listed as 124 Temple Street from 1837, the address taken over from John Milsom (qv) who moved to 56 Redcliff Street in about 1836 (the mention of 114 Temple Street in 1839 Robson is almost certainly an error). The partnership is occasionally listed as F. & E. Melsom, particularly in the Mathews directories of 1841 and 1842 and the Mathews classified list of stoneware potters thereafter. From 1860 to 1862 the firm is listed as Edward Melsom alone, and from 1863 until 1867 it appears as Francis Melsom alone. The Slater directory of 1868 lists Francis Melsom alone but also the partnership of Edward & Francis Melsom, which is presumably an editorial error. Francis Melsom's residence is given as 21 Cathay in 1856 Kelly and 1859 Harrison.

Throughout the firm's existence they are listed as stoneware manufacturers, with the improved white glazed stoneware first mentioned in 1846 Slater and brown stoneware listed until at least 1866. The manufacture of patent water pipes is last mentioned in 1864. An advertisement in 1865 Webster reads simply "Francis Melsom, improved white glazed and brown stone ware manufacturer, No. 124, Temple Street, Bristol".

Directory entries:

Mathews 1830–1867 NC, 1830–1867 PS
1839 Robson P
1846 Slater P
1848 Hunt PS
1850 Hunt PS
1850 Slater EM
1852 Scammell PS
1853 Scammell PS
1856 Kelly P
1857 Slater EM
1858 Slater EM
1859 Harrison BSW
1861 Kelly SM
1863 Kelly SM
1865 Webster EM
1865 Webster SM
1866 Harrod EM
1866 Harrod SM
1866 Kelly SM
1867 Morris SM
1868 Slater EM
1868 Slater NC

FRANCIS MELSOM,
IMPROVED WHITE GLAZED
AND
BROWN STONE WARE
MANUFACTURER,
No. 124, Temple Street,
BRISTOL.

Francis Melsom. *A typically concise advertisement which appeared in Webster's directory of 1865.*

Meredith, John
Meredith, John, & Son
Meredith, A. & J.
Meredith, Abraham
Meredith, William

Quay (1785–1808); 3 Trinity Street (1798–1801); St Philip's (1807–1812)

John Meredith is listed as a potter with a Staffordshire warehouse on the Quay in 1787 Bailey, but other early directories list only his business as a wholesale earthenware dealer. The address is sometimes given as number 33 or 35 on the Quay. A second address at 3 Trinity Street is added from 1798, and in 1801 the description reads "wholesale earthenware and bottled liquor warehouse". From 1803 to 1806 the style is given as John Meredith & Son and the manufacture of bricks and tiles is added. From 1807 the style reverts to just John Meredith and the manufacture of bricks and tiles is listed at St Philip's. Meredith's residence is listed as both Barton Hill and 13 College Street in 1807 and 1808, and as Castle Green in 1809, when the wholesale business on the Quay appears to have been discontinued.

From 1810 to 1812 the style is given as A. & J. Meredith, brick and tile manufacturers at St Philip's, and from 1813 this business also appears to have been discontinued, with Abraham Meredith listed only as a merchant. The only other relevant entry is for William Meredith, listed as a glass, china and earthenware dealer at the head of the Quay in 1816 Evans.

Directory entries:
Mathews 1793–1813 NC
1785 Browne NC 1792 Universal NC 1809 Holden NC 1816 Evans GCED
1787 Bailey NC

Milsom, John
Milsom & Melsom

124 Temple Street (1822–1836); 56 Redcliff Street (1836–1840)

John Milsom is first listed as a stoneware potter in 1822 Mathews, although an entry in 1821 for John Melsom (sic) with no trade given and the address as 122 Temple Street probably also relates to him. Between 1823 and 1826 he traded in partnership as Milsom & Melsom, but thereafter he reverted to trading alone. He is listed as a stoneware potter and patent water pipe manufacturer until 1840, although his address is given as 56 Redcliff Street from 1836. There is some confusion in the directories with the surname; it is sometimes listed in error as Melsom, Melson, or Milson.

Directory entries:
Mathews 1821–1840, 1823–1840 PS
1824 Pigot P 1830 Pigot P 1839 Robson P

Mineard, William

See: Maynard, William

Moorse, John F.

Albert Pottery, York Street, St Philip's Marsh

John F. Moorse was the manager of the Albert Pottery Co. at St Philip's Marsh from 1875 to at least 1906. He has an individual entry as such in 1906 Sharp.

Directory entries:
1906 Sharp P

Morgan & Hawley
Cornwallis Pottery, Stapleton Road
Morgan & Hawley were manufacturers of earthenware, porcelain, and sanitary goods, and worked the Cornwallis Pottery in Stapleton Road. They are listed only in 1857 Slater and the Mathews directories of 1857 and 1858. They appear to have been succeeded by Mayer & Co. (qv).
Directory entries:
Mathews 1857–1858 P, 1858 NC
1857 Slater EM

Morgan, Walker & Co.
Thomas Street
Morgan, Walker & Co. are listed as brown stone ware manufacturers at Thomas Street in 1807 Mathews.
Directory entries:
Mathews 1807 NC

N

Nelson, Isaac
9 Black-Fryars
Isaac Nelson was not a potter but is listed as a china mender at 9 Black-Fryars in 1775 Sketchley.
Directory entries:
1775 Sketchley NC

Niblett, Alfred
Queen Ann Street, Barton Hill, St Philip's
Alfred Niblett is first listed as a manufacturer of brown ware at Barton Hill in 1866 Kelly and similar entries appear in other directories through to 1888, although he is described as a red ware pottery manufacturer in 1876 Morris. His name is misprinted as Arthur in one entry in 1880 Slater. He does not appear in the Mathews and Wright directories until 1871, and thereafter the listings are erratic. He is classified as a potter from 1871 to 1875 and again from 1884 to 1886, and as a stoneware manufacturer and dealer from 1879 through to 1890. In the alphabetical entries he is listed between 1871 and 1890, but there are no entries in 1875 and 1876, and again between 1887 and 1889. The factory is sometimes described as the Barton Hill Pottery, and Niblett's address is given as 3 Queen Ann Street, with no trade listed, in 1890 Wright.
Directory entries:
Wright 1871–1874 NC, 1877–1886 NC, 1890 NC, 1871–1875 P, 1884–1886 P, 1879–1890 SMD

1866 Kelly EM	1870 Kelly EM	1879 Kelly BWM	1883 Kelly BWM
1868 Slater EM	1875 Kelly BWM	1880 Slater EM	1885 Kelly BWM
1869 Bristol NC	1876 Morris PSM	1880 Slater NC	1888 Bennett EM

Niblett, Arthur
See: Niblett, Alfred

Norgrove, W.
See: Butcher, William, & Co.

Oakley, John
Okely, Martha
Okely, Martha, & Son
Okely, William
Okely, William, & Co.
Lewins Mead (1793–1805); Under the Bank (1806–1821); Redcliff Back (1822–1823); St John's Bridge (1827)

William Okely is listed as a brown stone potter at Redcliff Back with a retail shop at Redcliff Hill in the Mathews directories of 1822 and 1823, but he was trading much earlier as a tobacco pipe maker. The family name first appears between 1793 and 1798 when John Oakley (or Oakely) is listed as a tobacco pipe maker at Lewins Mead. He was succeeded by his widow, Martha Oakley, in 1799, and she is listed through to 1805 although the name is shown as Okely from 1801. The firm then moved to an address listed as under the Bank and became Martha Okely & Son, with entries from 1806 to 1812, with a residence shown as Host Street from 1810. From 1813 the firm is shown as William Okely who is described as a "tobacco pipe manufacturer and importer of tobacco pipe and potters' clays". He traded alone until 1816, and this was followed by a short period when the style was William Okely & Co., listed 1817 to 1819. In the Evans directories of 1817 and 1818 the clay merchant business is listed at No. 9 Tontine Warehouse. From 1820 entries again show William Okely trading alone.

In 1822 and 1823 the address is listed as Redcliff Back with a retail shop at Redcliff Hill; this is the period when the manufacture of brown stone pottery is mentioned (both by Mathews and in 1822 Pigot). Following three years when the firm is not listed by Mathews, there is one more entry in 1827, once again only as a tobacco pipe manufacturer and importer of tobacco pipe and potters' clay, but at St John's Bridge. Okely's residence is shown as Host Street until 1820, and then as Kington's Buildings in 1821 and Neyler's Cottages at Horfield in 1827. In the later years the surname is mostly listed as Okely, although variants such as Okeley occasionally appear.

Directory entries:
Mathews 1793–1823 NC, 1827 NC, 1823 PS
1816 Evans TPM 1817 Evans TPM 1818 Evans TPM 1822 Pigot P

Oland, John
St Philip's Marsh (1821–1826); near Hillsbridge (1823); 2 Langton Terrace (1824)

John Oland is listed as a potter at various addresses between 1821 and 1826. He appears first at St Philip's Marsh in 1821 Mathews and 1822 Pigot, then near Hillsbridge in 1823 Mathews, at 2 Langton Terrace in 1824 Mathews and 1824 Pigot, and finally at St Philip's again in the Mathews directories for 1825 and 1826, but only in the classified section. All the entries describe him as a brown stone potter

or manufacturer of stoneware. His residence is listed as 12 Lodge Street in 1821 Mathews, and an earlier individual entry in 1818 at 1 Somerset Street, Redcliff Meads, which lists no trade, may also be relevant.
Directory entries:
Mathews 1818 NC, 1821 NC, 1823–1824 NC, 1821 PS, 1823 PS, 1825–1826 PS
1822 Pigot P 1824 Pigot P

Oppenheim, Israel
See: Woodville Pottery Co.

Organ, Daniel
Leek Lane
Daniel Organ is listed at Leek Lane in the Mathews directories between 1809 and 1811, described as a "manufacturer of brown stone ware, melting–pots, &c."
Directory entries:
Mathews 1809–1811 NC

P

Pardoe, Thomas
Under the Bank (1809–1811); 28 Bath Street (1812–1816); Thomas Street (1820–1822)
Thomas Pardoe was a china enameller, not a potter, and makes his first appearance in 1809 Mathews. His address is listed as under the Bank, and it seems possible that he had some connection with John Eaves (qv), also listed as a china enameller at that address between 1807 and 1809. Pardoe is described as a "china enameller & gilder, wholesale & retail" from 1810, and his address is given as 28 Bath Street from 1812. There is a break in the Mathews entries between 1817 and 1819, although he is still listed in 1818 Evans, and from 1820 his address is shown as Long Row, Thomas Street. Glass is first mentioned in 1813, and the entries from 1820 describe him as a glass stainer, with no explicit mention of china. Godden states that Pardoe left Bristol and was at Nantgarw from about 1821 and that he died in 1823.
Directory entries:
Mathews 1809–1816 NC, 1820–1822 NC
1811 Holden NC 1816 Evans GCED 1817 Evans GStain 1818 Evans CGEn
1816 Evans ChinaE 1817 Evans CGEn 1817 Evans GCED 1818 Evans GStain

Pardoe, William Henry
Pardoe, Henry & Charles
Pardoe, Charles & George
Avon Street, St Philip's
William Henry Pardoe is classified as a stoneware potter in the Mathews directories of 1847 and 1848 only, although the alphabetical entries list him at Avon Street, St Philip's, from 1847 through to 1866. He is also listed as a potter in 1848 Hunt and as a stoneware potter in 1853 Scammell, although his main business seems to have been the manufacture of tobacco pipes. Brown ware garden pots are mentioned by

Mathews from 1860, and this is confirmed by the entries in 1865 Webster and 1866 Harrod which both mention brownware.

These last two directories also list the firm C. & G. Pardoe as "brown ware, tobacco pipe, and garden pot makers", and Charles and George Pardoe are also listed in 1863 Kelly with a similar description. The same entries appeared in 1861 Kelly under the names Henry and Charles Pardoe, but neither of these two family partnerships appear in the Mathews directories.

Directory entries:

Mathews 1847–1866 NC, 1847–1848 PS

1848 Hunt PS	1861 Kelly P	1865 Webster EM	1866 Harrod NC
1853 Scammell PS	1863 Kelly EM	1865 Webster NC	
1861 Kelly EM	1863 Kelly P	1866 Harrod EM	

Patience, Edward
Patience, Edward, & Co.

Temple Backs

Edward Patience & Co. are listed as brown stone potters at Temple Backs in 1803 Mathews and at Temple Street between 1805 and 1807. From 1808 until 1818 the address reverts to Temple Backs but the listings give Edward Patience alone, still described as a brown stone potter.

Directory entries:

Mathews 1803–1818 NC

1809 Holden NC	1816 Evans P	1818 Evans PS
1811 Holden NC	1817 Evans PS	

Patience & Gadd

Counter Slip

Patience & Gadd are listed as potters at Counter Slip in 1785 Browne. They were succeeded by Joseph Gadd & Co. (qv).

Directory entries:

1785 Browne NC

Patience, Thomas

139 Temple Street

Thomas Patience is listed as a victualler and potter at the Cross Keys, 139 Temple Street, in 1775 Sketchley. Although he is not listed elsewhere, the Cross Keys are mentioned in the Mathews directories between 1793 and 1799 under the name of Ann Patience, presumably his widow.

Directory entries:

1775 Sketchley NC

Pearce, Earl
Pearce, Elizabeth
Pearce & Quarman
Pearce, Thomas

Bread Street or Avon Street, St Philip's

The earliest appearance of the family name Pearce is in 1775 Sketchley where Edward Pearce (qv) is listed as a pipe maker, but the first potter is Earl Pearce, listed as a brown potter at St Philip's in 1792 Universal. He is also shown as a potter at Bread Street in the Mathews directories of 1793 and 1795. He was

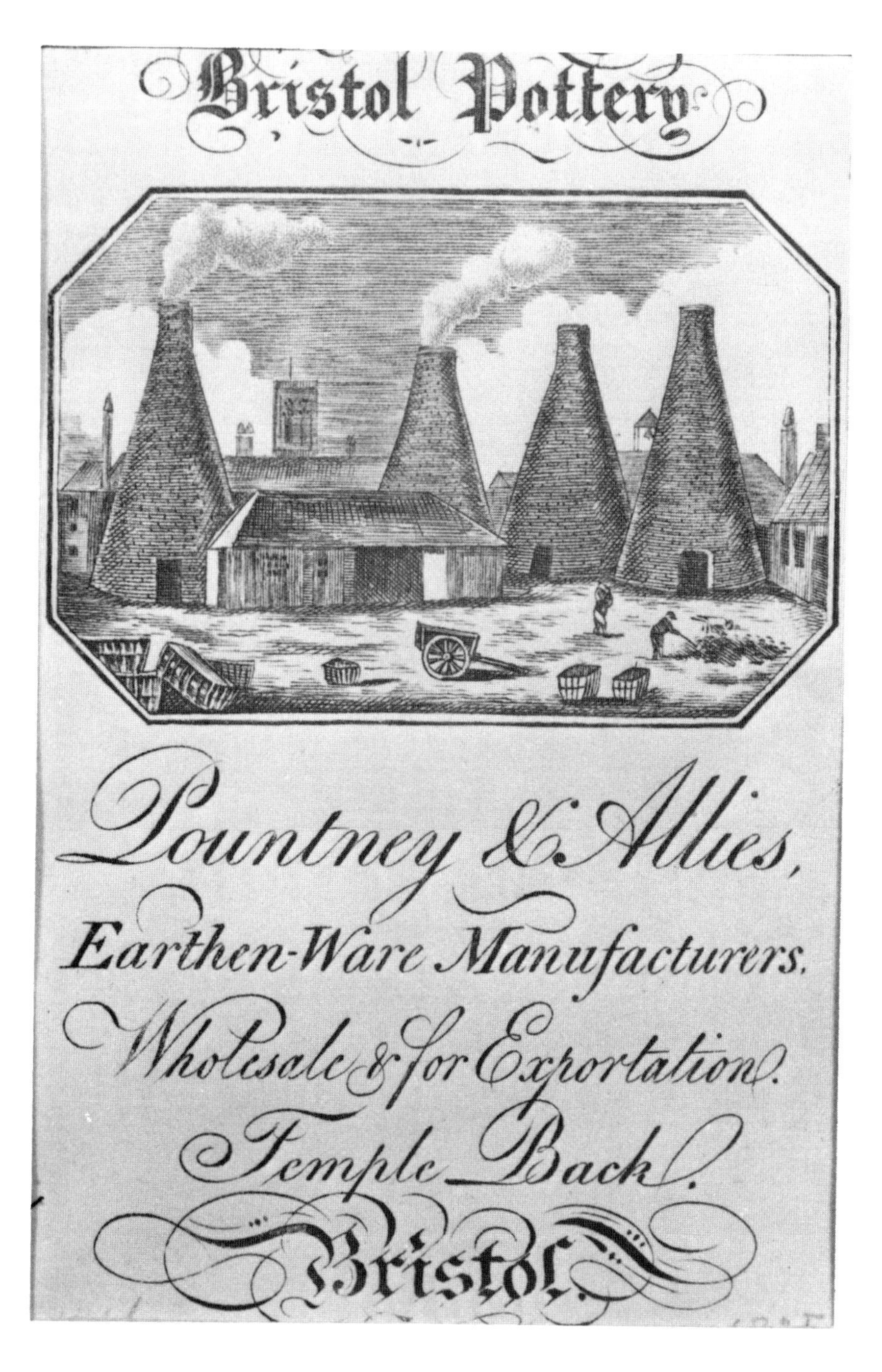

Pountney & Allies. *A trade card based on the earlier design used by Henry Carter & Co. and Carter & Pountney. (BMAG)*

Bristol Pottery 28th. April 1837.
TEMPLE BACK

Bot. of Pountney & Goldney.
(Earthen Ware Manufacturers.)

Returnd Crates not allowd for until received

WHOLESALE & FOR EXPORTATION.

	£	s	d
One breakfast & tea set. Green London Sprig Containing			
12 Pr. breakfast cups & S.	.	4	6
12 coffee cups 7/- & 12 Pr. tea Cups & S. 2/6	.	4	6
6 Egg cups.	.	1	-
2 Teapots — 18/- 24/9	.	1	9
1 cream		.	4
4 bowls. 2 slop 2 sugar.	.	1	-
16 plates 4 9/- 12 6 in 7/-	.	3	-
1 butter tub	.	1	6
1 coffee pot	.	2	-
3 milk Jugs.	.	1	-
2 blue Jugs.	.	1	6
6 ½ pint mugs.	.	1	6
6 dishes. 2 9/9 2 10/7/- 2 12/P	.	3	-
1 Ewer & bason. Green coral		3	6
1 brush tray do	.	1	-
1 soap box do	.	1	-
3 paint slabs.	.	1	-
9 dishes. 2 10 9/- 2 12 7/6 2 14 2/6 2 16 9/- 18 3/6 Abby	.	10	-
	2	3	1

Pountney & Goldney. *An invoice for a breakfast and tea set together with some toilet wares and 'three paint slabs', dated 28 April 1837. (BMAG)*

succeeded by Elizabeth Pearce, presumably his widow, who is listed at Avon Street in 1797 and 1798, Bread Street in 1799 and 1801, and at Avon Street again between 1803 and 1814. There was also a partnership listed as Pearce & Quarman at Bread Street in 1797 and 1798. Elizabeth Pearce was in turn succeeded by Thomas Pearce making brown ware pottery at Avon Street, listed only in 1816.

Directory entries:
Mathews 1793–1814 NC, 1816 NC
1792 Universal NC 1809 Holden NC 1811 Holden NC

Pearce, Edward
8 Halliers Lane

Edward Pearce is listed as a pipe maker at Halliers Lane in 1775 Sketchley, presumably referring to tobacco pipes rather than water or drain pipes.

Directory entries:
1775 Sketchley NC

Phillips, James
See: James, Philip

Pinker, Henry
Alfred Parade, Marlborough Hill, Kingsdown

Henry Pinker is classified as a potter at 8 Alfred Parade in 1842 Pigot but this is clearly an error. He appears as a plasterer and tiler in the Mathews directories between 1823 and 1833, and thereafter as a plasterer and painter until 1853. The address is listed as 7 Alfred Parade until 1835, but as number 8 from 1840.

Directory entries:
Mathews 1823–1853 NC
1842 Pigot P

Pountney & Allies
Pountney & Goldney
Pountney, J.D.
Pountney, J.D., & Co.
Pountney, Edwards & Co.
Water Lane, Temple Back

The Pountney & Allies partnership succeeded Henry Carter & Co. at the Bristol Pottery and is listed in directories between 1816 and 1835. The entry in 1817 Mathews describes them as "manufacturers of printed, painted, enamelled and cream-coloured earthenware", but the later entries read "for the manufacture of all sorts of plain and ornamental earthenware". They were succeeded for a very short period by J. D. Pountney trading alone, listed only in 1836 Mathews, and then by Pountney & Goldney who appear in directories from 1837 to 1850. The only directory to give additional information is 1846 Slater which lists the manager as Samuel Marsh. The Pountney & Goldney partnership was again succeeded by J.D. Pountney trading alone, listed between 1851 and 1853.

John Decimus Pountney died on 30th December 1852 and the firm was continued by his widow, Charlotte, and is listed as J.D. Pountney & Co. between 1854 and 1857. This was followed by the brief and little-recorded partnership of Pountney,

Edwards & Co., which appears only in the alphabetical list in 1858 Mathews. The firm then continued as Pountney & Co. (see below).

Directory entries:

Mathews 1817–1858 NC, 1820–1821 P, 1823–1853 P

1816 Evans ECM
1817 Evans ECM
1818 Evans ECM
1822 Pigot P
1824 Pigot P
1830 Pigot P
1839 Robson P
1842 Pigot P
1846 Slater P
1848 Hunt PS
1850 Hunt PS
1850 Slater EM
1852 Scammell PS
1853 Scammell PS
1856 Kelly NC
1857 Slater EM

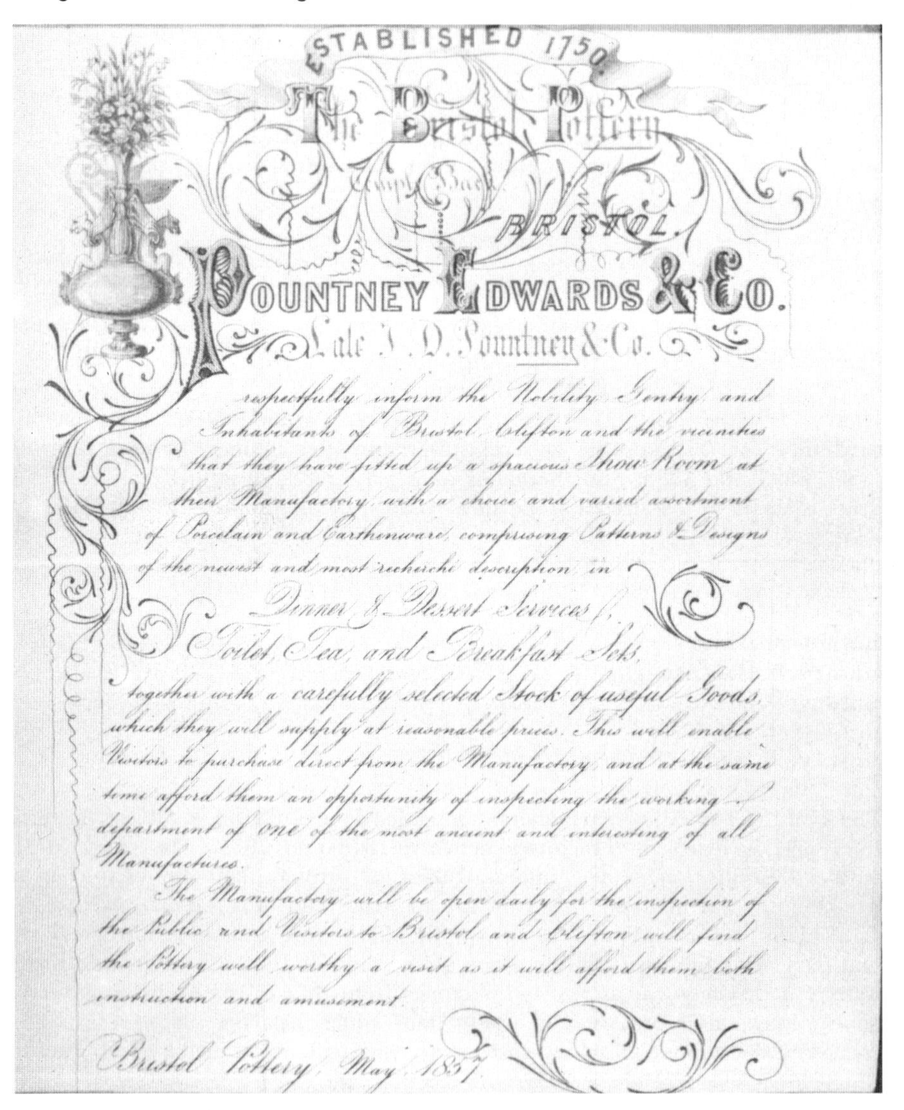

ESTABLISHED 1750
The Bristol Pottery
Temple Back
BRISTOL.
POUNTNEY EDWARDS & CO.
Late J. D. Pountney & Co.

respectfully inform the Nobility Gentry and Inhabitants of Bristol Clifton and the vicinities that they have fitted up a spacious Show Room at their Manufactory with a choice and varied assortment of Porcelain and Earthenware, comprising Patterns & Designs of the newest and most recherché description in

Dinner & Dessert Services,
Toilet, Tea, and Breakfast Sets,

together with a carefully selected Stock of useful Goods, which they will supply at reasonable prices. This will enable Visitors to purchase direct from the Manufactory and at the same time afford them an opportunity of inspecting the working department of one of the most ancient and interesting of all Manufactures.

The Manufactory will be open daily for the inspection of the Public and Visitors to Bristol and Clifton will find the Pottery well worthy a visit as it will afford them both instruction and amusement.

Bristol Pottery, May 1857.

Pountney, Edwards & Co. *An announcement for this little-recorded partnership dated May 1857 inviting customers to visit a 'spacious Show Room' at the pottery. (BMAG)*

Pountney & Co.

Pountney & Co. Ltd.

Bristol Pottery, Water Lane, Temple Backs (until 1885); Victoria Pottery, Feeder Road, St Philip's Marsh (from 1873); Crown Pottery, St George's (1891)

Following the short lived partnership of Pountney, Edwards & Co. (see above), the Bristol Pottery traded under the simple style of Pountney & Co. The first directory entry is actually in 1854, in the Mathews classified section, although strictly this relates to J.D. Pountney & Co. The alphabetical list, which is generally more accurate, shows the new style first in 1859. It also appears in 1858 Slater. The address is given as 27 Temple Backs from 1871. The firm took over the Victoria Pottery at St Philip's Marsh which is listed from 1873, although the Bristol Pottery in Water Lane is still shown until 1885. The date of establishment is claimed as 1750 in 1875 Kelly.

The directories give little information on the products, continuing the earlier description "for the manufacture of plain and ornamental earthenware" in the Mathews directories until 1869, and describing the firm as "manufacturers of all kinds of blue and white earthenware" in 1865 Webster and 1866 Harrod. Otherwise the entries refer to the firm simply as "earthenware manufacturers". An advertisement in 1865 Webster is much more forthcoming and reads "Manufacturers of all kinds of blue and white earthenware, in toilet, dinner, and tea ware, of which a large assortment is always kept in stock. Initials and crests printed to order. Samples may be seen at the works. A large assortment of china always kept on hand. Cheap vases in every variety and other ornaments, in Parian, &c. P. and C. being the appointed agents of some of the largest manufacturers of these goods, are able to supply them on the most reasonable terms. This is the only blue & white earthenware manufactory within 90 miles of Bristol".

The firm is first listed as a limited company in 1889 Kelly, although this style does not appear in the Mathews directories until 1890. Showrooms at 8 Bath Street are listed in 1889 Kelly and 1891 Kelly, and the latter is the only directory to record the firm's ownership of the Crown Pottery at St George's. A completely new pottery was built at Causeway, Fishponds, early in the twentieth century, and the new factory is listed along with the old Victoria Pottery in 1905 Wright. The firm is listed as "late of Victoria Pottery" in 1906 Wright and only the new address is given in 1906 Sharp.

Directory entries:

Mathews 1859–1869 NC, 1854–1869 P

Wright 1870–1885 NC, 1887–1904 NC, 1870–1906 P

1858 Slater EM	1870 Kelly EM	1883 Kelly EM	1897 Kelly EM
1859 Harrison EM	1872 Morris PSM	1883 Kelly P	1899 Town P
1861 Kelly EM	1875 Kelly EM	1885 Kelly EM	1900 Town P
1863 Kelly EM	1875 Kelly P	1885 Kelly P	1901 Town P
1865 Webster EM	1876 Morris PSM	1888 Bennett EM	1902 Kelly EM
1866 Harrod EM	1878 Owen NC	1889 Bennett ED	1902 Town P
1866 Kelly EM	1879 Kelly EM	1889 Kelly P	1903 Town P
1868 Slater EM	1879 Kelly P	1891 Kelly P	1904 Sharp P
1869 Bristol NC	1880 Slater EM	1894 Kelly NC	1906 Sharp P

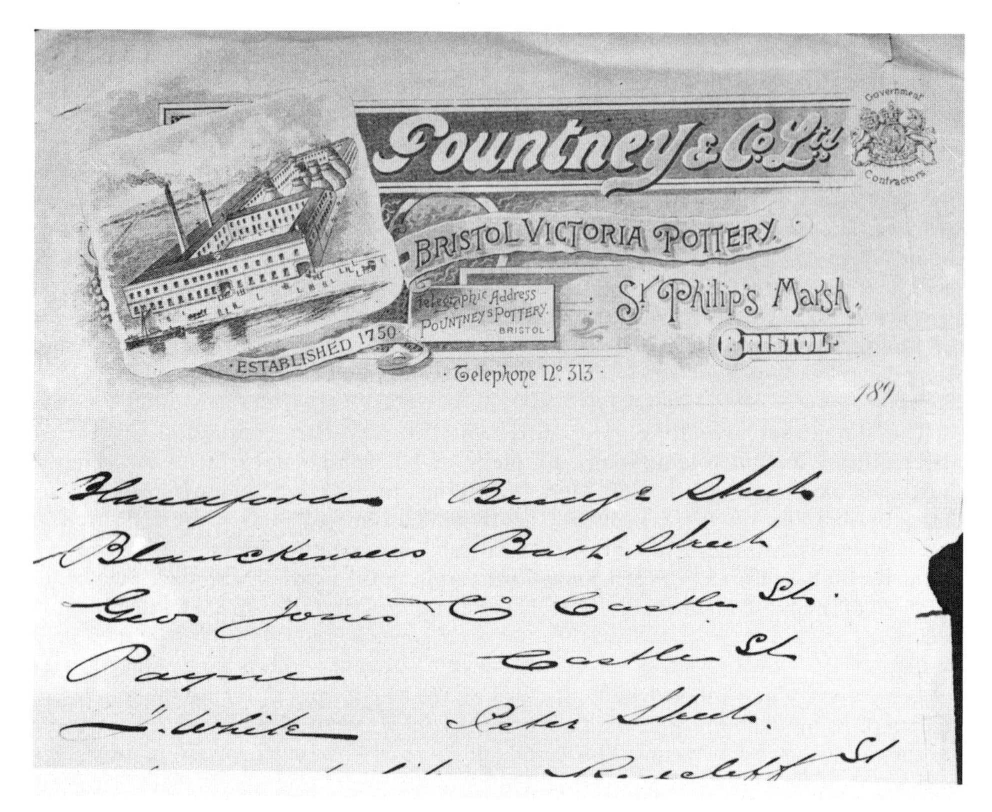

Pountney & Co. Ltd. *Invoice heading dating from the 1890s showing the Bristol Victoria Pottery at St Philip's Marsh. (BRO – reference 20165)*

Powell, William & Thomas
Powell, William & John
Powell, William
Powell, William, & Sons

Thomas Street (1816–1829); Temple Gate (from 1810)

William & Thomas Powell began their partnership with a Stourbridge glass warehouse in Bath Parade, Temple Gate, first listed in 1810. It is not clear whether there was any direct relationship with John Powell who is listed as a glass dealer at Bath Street between 1806 and 1811, and Elizabeth Powell who is similarly listed in the Evans directories of 1816 and 1817. William & Thomas Powell expanded to become brown stone potters with premises in Thomas Street, listed from 1816. They continued both businesses but the Thomas Street premises are not listed after 1829 when the pottery was moved to Temple Gate. The glass dealership was discontinued not long afterwards. They were succeeded by William & John Powell, listed in 1831 and 1832, and then by William Powell trading alone, listed from 1833 to 1854. The address is listed as 114 Temple Gate in 1839 Robson.

It was in 1828 that John, Thomas and William Powell, "glass merchants and stoneware manufacturers" of the city of Bristol, took out a patent for the manufacture of glazed stoneware sugar moulds. Patent number 5657 was granted on 17th May 1828 for "certain improvements in the process, machinery, or apparatus for forming, making, or producing moulds or vessels for refining sugar, and in the application of materials hitherto unused in making the said moulds". The first mention of the patent appears in 1831 Mathews, and thereafter entries refer to it along with the firm's stoneware activities until at least 1854.

From 1836 William Powell is described as "inventor and sole manufacturer of the improved stoneware, which is glazed inside and out with a glaze warranted to resist acids, and will not absorb". The reference to "sole manufacturer" disappears from 1847. The manufacture of glass bottles appears in 1839 Robson and some later directories, and a reference to "patent air-tight stoppered stoneware" appears in 1850 Slater.

From 1855 through to 1906 the firm is listed as William Powell & Sons, operating throughout from Temple Gate, although a pottery at Redcliff Mead Lane, Cathay, is also listed in 1904 Sharp and 1906 Sharp. The later entries continue to promote the firm's status as inventors and original manufacturers of "the improved stoneware" or "the celebrated Bristol Stoneware" and many concentrate on their stoneware jars and bottles. The firm is frequently listed simply as Powell & Sons, and references to Powell & Co. refer to the separate glass bottle manufacturing business in Avon Street. The style is misprinted as William Powell & Son in 1863 Kelly. The firm eventually amalgamated with Price, Sons & Co. (qv) and the new company is listed as Price, Powell & Co. from 1907.

William Powell & Sons advertised continuously in the Wright directories from 1872 to 1902. The earliest advertisements describe them simply as "inventors and original manufacturers of the improved stoneware" but they soon became much more descriptive and usually included engravings of either water filters or wicker covered stoneware jars.

Directory entries:
Mathews 1806–1869 NC, 1820–1821 PS, 1823–1869 PS
Wright 1870–1906 NC, 1870–1906 P, 1878–1893 SMD, 1894–1906 SJBM
1809 Holden NC
1816 Evans P
1816 Evans GCED
1817 Evans PS
1817 Evans GCED
1818 Evans PS
1818 Evans GCED
1822 Pigot P
1824 Pigot P
1830 Pigot P
1839 Robson P
1842 Pigot P
1846 Slater P
1848 Hunt PS
1850 Hunt PS
1850 Slater EM
1852 Scammell PS
1853 Scammell PS
1856 Kelly P
1857 Slater EM
1858 Slater EM
1861 Kelly SM
1863 Kelly SM
1865 Webster EM
1865 Webster SM
1866 Harrod EM
1866 Harrod SM
1866 Kelly SM
1867 Morris SM
1868 Slater EM
1869 Bristol NC
1870 Kelly SM
1872 Morris PSM
1875 Kelly SM
1876 Morris PSM
1879 Kelly SM
1880 Slater EM
1883 Kelly SM
1885 Kelly SM
1888 Bennett BM
1889 Bennett BM
1889 Kelly SJM
1889 Kelly SM
1891 Kelly SJM
1891 Kelly SM
1894 Kelly SJM
1894 Kelly SM
1897 Kelly SJM
1897 Kelly SM
1899 Town P
1900 Town P
1901 Town P
1902 Kelly SM
1902 Town P
1903 Town P
1903 Town SBJM
1904 Sharp BM
1904 Sharp P
1904 Sharp SJBM
1904 Sharp SMD
1906 Sharp BM
1906 Sharp P
1906 Sharp SJBM
1906 Sharp SMD

WM. POWELL & SONS,

Inventors and Original Manufacturers of the

Improved Stoneware,

TEMPLE GATE POTTERY, BRISTOL.

WILLIAM POWELL & SONS,

TEMPLE GATE POTTERY, BRISTOL.

INVENTORS AND ORIGINAL MANUFACTURERS OF THE

Improved Bristol Stoneware Spirit Jars (wickered & plain),

BARRELS, WATER FILTERS, EXPORT ALE AND PORTER BOTTLES, GINGER BEER BOTTLES,

BUTTER POTS (COVERED AND UNCOVERED),

Jam, Pickle, Mustard, and Salt Jars, Churns, and especial Registered Air-tight Pot.

WILLIAM POWELL & SONS do not send Specimens to Exhibitions, preferring to rely upon the general excellence of their Ware.

BRISTOL DIRECTORY ADVERTISING SHEET, 1886. 65A

WILLIAM POWELL & SONS,

Temple Gate Pottery,

BRISTOL.

Inventors and Original Manufacturers of the Improved Bristol Stone Ware.

Jars and Bottles (wickered and plain), Barrels, Water Filters, Spittoons, Ale, Porter, and Ginger-Beer Bottles, Drip Pans and Buckets, Pickling and Preserve, Butter Jars, Syrup Pans, Jam, Mustard and Salt Jars, Brunswick Black and Polish Bottles, Churns, Jugs, Battery Cells, and an especial registered Air-Tight Pot.

W. P. & SONS do not send specimens to Exhibitions, preferring to rely upon the general excell nce of their WARE.

William Powell & Sons. *Three typical advertisements from a series in the Wright directories which appeared from 1872 onwards. These three date from 1872, 1881 and 1886. (BRL)*

50A BRISTOL DIRECTORY ADVERTISING SHEET, 1890.

IMPROVED GLAZED SPIRIT JARS.

WILLIAM POWELL & SONS

Inventors and Original Manufacturers of the

BRISTOL STONE WARE.

SPIRIT, TREACLE, & VINEGAR JARS
(Wickered and Plain),
DRIP PANS, BARRELS, STONE WARE
ALE, PORTER, AND GINGER BEER
BOTTLES.
IMPROVED WATER FILTERS, JUGS,
PANS, PICKLING & PRESERVE JARS,
And an ESPECIAL REGISTERED AIR-
TIGHT POT.

WILLIAM POWELL & SONS have introduced a new and effective way of marking Name and Trade Mark, &c., on Jars in Colour.

Specimens may be had upon application to

TEMPLE GATE POTTERY, BRISTOL.

BRISTOL DIRECTORY ADVERTISING SHEET, 1901. 51A

IMPROVED GLAZED SPIRIT JARS.

WILLIAM POWELL & SONS

Inventors and Original Manufacturers of the

BRISTOL STONE WARE

SPIRIT, TREACLE, and VINEGAR JARS
(Wickered and Plain).
DRIP PANS, BARRELS, STONE WARE, ALE,
PORTER, and GINGER BEER BOTTLES.
IMPROVED WATER FILTERS, JUGS, PANS,
PICKLING and PRESERVE JARS, and an
ESPECIAL REGISTERED AIR TIGHT POT.

WM. POWELL & SONS have introduced a new and effective way of marking Name and Trade Mark, &c., on Jars in colour.

Specimens may be had upon application to

TEMPLE GATE POTTERY, BRISTOL.

William Powell & Sons. *Two more advertisements from the Wright directories, these dating from 1890 and 1901. (BRL)*

Price, Charles
Price, Charles, & Son
Price, Charles, & Sons
Price, Charles & Joseph Read
Price, Joseph & Charles, & Brothers
Price, Sons & Co.

Temple Street; Thomas Street; St Philip's; Victoria Street

Charles Price succeeded Price & Read (qv) and is listed as a brown stone potter at 123 Temple Street and next to the Bunch of Grapes in Thomas Street between 1818 and 1822. His firm continued until about 1960 and is listed in virtually all the directories although there were many changes of style and addresses. According to the Mathews alphabetical lists the sequence was Charles Price (1818–1822), Charles Price & Son (1823–1842), Charles Price & Sons (1843–1849), Charles & Joseph Read Price (1850–1863), Joseph & Charles Price & Brothers (1864–1883), Price, Sons & Co. (1884–1906), and subsequently Price, Powell & Co. (qv). The dates listed in the Mathews classified entries and other directories vary slightly. The styles are occasionally abbreviated to Price Brothers (Wright 1871–1884, 1876 Morris, and 1878 Owen) or Price & Sons (1889 Bennett). Entries for Price, Sons & Co. in the Wright directories between 1885 and 1902 claim that the firm was established in 1740, and list prize medals that they were awarded at the exhibitions at Paris in 1867, Philadelphia in 1876, and Sydney in 1880.

The firm occupied a variety of addresses in Temple Street (listed only until 1875), St Philip's (1827–1844), Victoria Street (1873–1887), and Thomas Street (throughout the period). The directories are consistent in listing the Victoria Street address as number 69, usually described as offices, but sometimes rather misleadingly as "The Old Stoneware Potteries" (e.g. 1880 Slater). There is, however, considerable variation in the directory listings of the addresses in both Thomas Street and Temple Street, the earliest and latest appearances being:

Address	Dates	Address	Dates
37 Thomas Street	1856–1875	42 Thomas Street	1866–1906
38 Thomas Street	1855–1875	43 Thomas Street	1827–1906
39 Thomas Street	1855–1906	44 Thomas Street	1869–1906
40 Thomas Street	1887–1906	45 Thomas Street	1887–1906
41 Thomas Street	1887–1906		
123 Temple Street	1818–1859	131 Temple Street	1854–1869
125 Temple Street	1827–1869	135 Temple Street	1839–1841
130 Temple Street	1863–1868	136 Temple Street	1842–1853

In addition, probable misprints include 12 Temple Street (1858 Slater), 43 Temple Street (1858 Slater), 114 Temple Street (1839 Robson), and 14 Thomas Street (1872 Morris and 1876 Morris).

Early descriptions list the firms simply as brown stone potters, with particular mention of patent water pipes between 1825 and 1852. The first mention of the improved "or highly glazed stoneware" is in 1845, and thereafter the firms are invariably described simply as stoneware or improved stoneware manufacturers, or as manufacturers of every description of stoneware (1880 Slater). An advertisement in 1865 Webster mentions only improved stoneware, but another in 1880 Slater includes the description "manufacturers of the far-famed Bristol stoneware, glazed inside and out with a vitrified enamel; spirit jars; pickling and preserve jars; screw or stoppered jars; export jam, mustard, and salt jars; ink bottles; ginger beer bottles; ale and porter bottles; jars cased in wickerwork; charcoal water filters; cocoa pans, and every description of stoneware for domestic use''. Similarly worded advertisements also appear in the Wright directories from 1878 through to 1906 and most of the Kelly's directories from 1879, although these usually include an engraving showing samples of the firm's stonewares. Later versions also mention insulators and battery jars.

Members of the Price family who were partners in the firm are often listed individually with their residences. Alfred N. Price is listed in 1864 Mathews, at Bassein Villa, Cotham Road in 1867 Morris and 1869 Bristol, and at Fern Hollow, Sneyd Park in 1880 Slater. His second name is given as Newell in 1867 Morris. Charles Price is listed at Linton Villa, Richmond Park or Pembroke Road, in 1859 Harrison and 1869 Bristol. Joseph Read Price is listed at Berkeley Villa, Ashley Hill in 1859 Harrison, at Inkerman Villa, Tyndall's Park, Clifton in 1867 Morris and 1869 Bristol, and at Woodgrove House, Westfield park, Redland in 1880 Slater. Samuel N. Price is listed at 2 Cotham Grove in 1867 Morris and 1869 Bristol, and at 20 Redland Park Villas in 1880 Slater. His second name is listed as Newman in 1867 Morris but as Newell in 1869 Mathews.

Directory entries:

Mathews 1818–1869 NC, 1820–1821 PS, 1823–1869 PS

Wright 1870–1906 NC, 1870–1906 P, 1871–1893 SMD, 1894–1906 SJBM

1818 Evans NC
1822 Pigot P
1824 Pigot P
1830 Pigot P
1839 Robson P
1839 Robson SW
1842 Pigot P
1846 Slater P
1848 Hunt PS
1850 Hunt PS
1850 Slater EM
1852 Scammell PS
1853 Scammell PS
1856 Kelly P
1857 Slater EM
1858 Slater EM
1859 Harrison BSW
1861 Kelly SM
1863 Kelly P
1863 Kelly SM
1865 Webster EM
1865 Webster SM
1866 Harrod EM
1866 Harrod SM
1866 Kelly P
1866 Kelly SM
1867 Morris P
1867 Morris SM
1868 Slater EM
1869 Bristol NC
1870 Kelly SM
1872 Morris PSM
1875 Kelly SM
1876 Morris PSM
1878 Owen SM
1879 Kelly SM
1880 Slater EM
1883 Kelly SM
1885 Kelly SM
1888 Bennett EM
1889 Bennett BM
1889 Bennett ED
1889 Kelly SM
1891 Kelly SM
1894 Kelly SM
1897 Kelly SM
1899 Town P
1900 Town P
1901 Town P
1902 Kelly SM
1902 Town P
1903 Town P
1903 Town SBJM
1904 Sharp BM
1904 Sharp P
1904 Sharp SJBM
1904 Sharp SMD
1906 Sharp BM
1906 Sharp P
1906 Sharp SJBM
1906 Sharp SMD

PRIZE MEDAL PARIS, 1867. AMERICAN CENTENNIAL, 1876.

J. & C. PRICE & BROTHERS,

OLD STONE WARE POTTERIES,

THOMAS ST. and VICTORIA ST., BRISTOL.

ILLUSTRATED PRICE LISTS ON APPLICATION.

Joseph & Charles Price & Brothers. *One of a series of advertisements which appeared in the Wright directories from 1878 onwards, this example dating from 1880. (BRL)*

PRICE, SONS, & COMPANY,

The Old Stoneware Potteries,

ESTABLISHED 1740. BRISTOL. OFFICES: 69, VICTORIA STREET.

Manufacturers of their far-famed **BRISTOL STONEWARE** (glazed inside and out with a vitrified enamel).

Spirit Jars, Pickling and Preserve Jars, Stoppered Jars for Acids. Water Filters, Ink Bottles, Export Jam, Mustard and Salt Jars Drug Jars, Ginger Beer Bottles, Ale and Porter Bottles for Exporting. Jars of all kinds cased in Wicker Work. Covered Jars, &c.

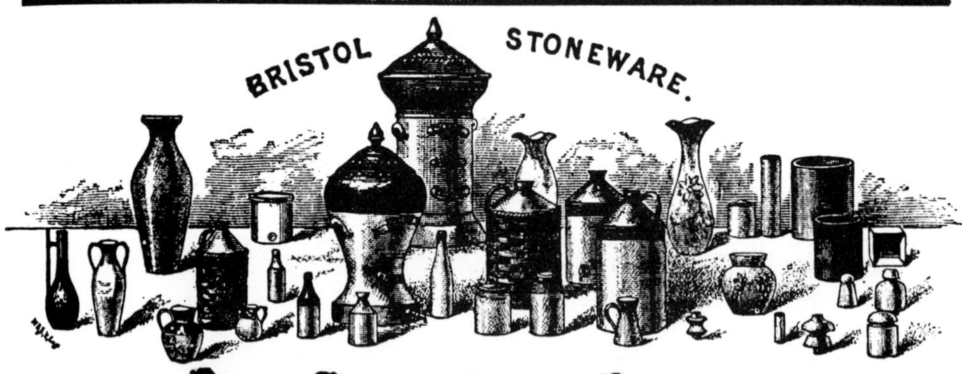

PRICE, SONS & COMPY. BRISTOL

PRIZE MEDALS. — LONDON. PARIS. PHILADELPHIA AND SYDNEY.

Manufacturers of their far-famed **BRISTOL STONEWARE** (glazed inside and out with a vitrified enamel).

Spirit Jars, Pickling and Preserve Jars, Stoppered Jars for Acids. Water Filters, Ink Bottles, Export Jam, Mustard and Salt Jars, Drug Jars, Ginger Beer Bottles, Ale and Porter Bottles for Exporting. Jars of all kinds cased in Wicker Work. Covered Jars, &c.

Price, Sons & Co. *Two typical advertisements from the Kelly directories, these appeared in 1883 and 1889. (TLH)*

BRISTOL DIRECTORY ADVERTISING SHEET, 1890. 47A

THE NEW REDCLIFFE ART WARE, PLAIN AND DECORATED.

ADMIRABLY ADAPTED FOR PAINTING. REQUIRES NO SECOND FIRING.

PRICE, SONS, & COMPANY,
THE OLD STONEWARE POTTERIES,
BRISTOL.

MANUFACTURERS OF HIGHLY GLAZED VITRIFIED BRISTOL STONEWARE.

Jars and Bottles of all kinds for Spirit Merchants, Grocers, Druggists, etc.

Ale, Porter and Ginger Beer Bottles.

INK BOTTLES, JAM, SALT, AND MUSTARD JARS,
AND EVERY VARIETY OF ARTICLE MADE IN STONEWARE.

ELECTRICAL STONEWARE. HIGHLY GLAZED INSULATORS·
Specially Strong Battery Jars, Primary and Secondary.
CHARCOAL WATER FILTERS, VARIOUS SHAPES, ALSO CISTERN FILTERS.

OFFICES & WORKS:—39, 40, 41, 42, 43, 44, & 45, ST. THOMAS ST. BRISTOL.

Established 1740. Offices and Works: ST. THOMAS STREET.

PRICE, SONS & CO.,
The Old Stoneware Potteries, BRISTOL.

MANUFACTURERS OF

Stone Bottles and Jars

OF ALL DESCRIPTIONS FOR SPIRITS, VINEGAR, BEER, &c.

Water Filters, Syrup Pans, Ink Bottles, Stone Bottles for Brewed Ginger Beer, Ale and Porter Bottles, &c.,

Highly Glazed Stoneware Insulators, and Battery Jars; Also Porous Cells, &c.

PRICE LISTS AND SAMPLES ON APPLICATION.

Nat. Telephone 279. Telegraphic Address, "PRICE, BRISTOL."

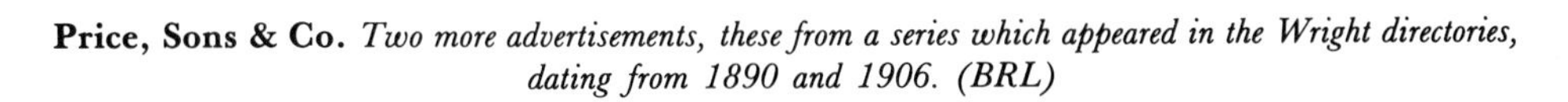

Price, Sons & Co. *Two more advertisements, these from a series which appeared in the Wright directories, dating from 1890 and 1906. (BRL)*

Price, Powell & Co.
Thomas Street

Although strictly outside the scope of this work, Price, Powell & Co. are included here for completeness. The firm was formed by the amalgamation of Price, Sons & Co. (see above) and William Powell & Sons (qv), the two largest Bristol stoneware factories. They are first listed in the Wright directory of 1907, and entries continue until 1960. They do not appear in 1962. The first advertisement for the combined firm appeared in 1907 Wright, promoting particularly "Tripoli" porous stone filters.

Directory entries:
Wright 1907 NC

Price, Powell & Co. *The first advertisement for the combined Price and Powell firm, copied from Wright's directory of 1907. (BRL)*

Price & Read
Temple Street; Thomas Street (from 1809)

Price & Read are listed as brown stone potters at Temple Street in the Mathews directories between 1799 and 1817, and also at Thomas Street from 1809. The Thomas Street address is listed as "next to the Bunch of Grapes" but three different addresses in Temple Street are given; number 124 (1799–1803), number 123 which is noted as "late Alsop" (1805–1809), and number 132 (1810–1817). The last of these also appears in the Evans directories of 1816 to 1818. The second partner's name is sometimes printed as Reed. The partnership was succeeded by Charles Price (qv) trading alone.

Directory entries:
Mathews 1799–1817 NC

1805 Holden NC	1811 Holden NC	1817 Evans PS
1809 Holden NC	1816 Evans P	1818 Evans PS

R

Reed, Charles
3 Counter Slip
Charles Reed is listed as a potter at 3 Counter Slip in 1775 Sketchley.
Directory entries:
1775 Sketchley NC

Reed, Joseph
Barrs Street
Joseph Reed is listed as a potter at Barrs Street in 1803 Mathews.
Directory entries:
Mathews 1803 NC

Reed, Joseph, & Co.
Temple Street
Joseph Reed & Co. are listed as potters at Temple Street in the Bailey directories of 1783 and 1784.
Directory entries:
1783 Bailey NC 1784 Bailey NC

Rich, William
Rich, John
Rich & Boon
Rich, Samuel
Rich (Mrs.)
Albert Road, St Philip's Marsh
The Rich family operated as potters in Albert Road, St Philip's Marsh, but the entries in the directories are confusing. According to the classified lists of potters in the Wright directories, the sequence was William Rich (listed 1871–1873), John Rich (1874–1875), Rich & Boon (1876–1877), John Rich and Samuel Rich (both listed in 1878), and finally Mrs. Rich, presumably a widow (1879–1883). Unfortunately the alphabetical entries differ, giving William Rich as a drain pipe and fire brick maker from 1850 to 1873 and again from 1875 to 1877, Rich & Boon as drain pipe makers from 1874 to 1878, and John Rich as a potter from 1879 to 1880. John Rich is also listed individually with no trade given from 1871 to 1874. There is no mention of Mrs. Rich, and after 1880 John Rich is still listed but described as a grocer and not a potter. Other directories simply confirm the existence of William Rich, listed in 1869 Bristol and 1872 Morris.
Directory entries:
Mathews 1850–1869 NC
Wright 1870–1880 NC, 1871–1883 P
1869 Bristol NC 1872 Morris PSM

Ring, Elizabeth
Ring, Elizabeth, & Co.
9 Bridge Street (1808–1813); 8 High Street (1814–1834)

Elizabeth Ring, the wife of Joseph Ring I, is listed as an individual in the Mathews directories of 1795 at Hillgrove Street, and from 1798 to 1807 at 14 Bath Street, an address which was used as a retail outlet by the Bristol Pottery. She operated a separate china, glass and Staffordshire warehouse along with her two daughters, Elizabeth and Sophia, and when she died in February 1816 her share of this business was left to the daughters. The business traded as Elizabeth Ring at 9 Bridge Street (listed 1808 to 1813) and then at 8 High Street (listed from 1814). Her residence is shown as 3 Guinea Street in 1812–1813, then as the old warehouse premises at 9 Bridge Street until 1816, and subsequently at 20 Stoke's Croft, presumably this address relating to the younger Elizabeth Ring.

From 1818 through to 1834 the business is shown as Elizabeth Ring & Co., the later entries reading ''extensive ware rooms for Stourbridge glass, china & Staffordshire ware, and agents, for Robins's royal filters, and Gibson's medical spoons''. The business was continued by Ring & Hood (listed 1835–1848), then by Charles Ring (listed 1849–1860). An entry in 1859 claims that the business was established in 1786.

Directory entries:
Mathews 1795 NC, 1798–1834 NC
1809 Holden NC 1816 Evans GCED 1818 Evans GCED
1811 Holden NC 1817 Evans GCED

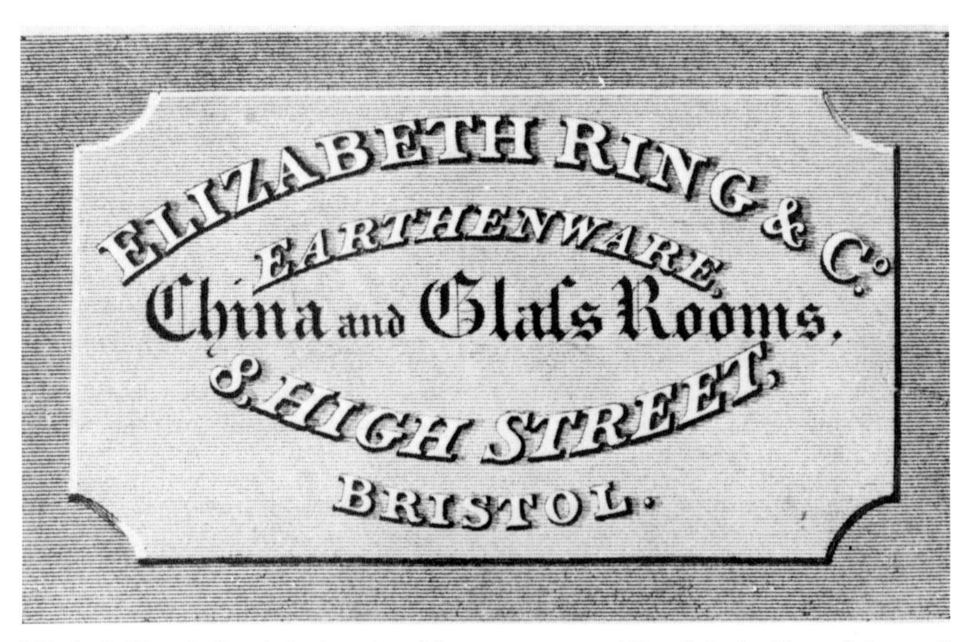

Elizabeth Ring & Co. *A simple trade card by an engraver named Burnell for the china and glass retail shop at 8 High Street. (BMAG)*

Ring, George
4 Avon Street, Temple

George Ring is classified as a potter at 4 Avon Street, Temple, in the Wright directories between 1871 and 1875, but these dates are inconsistent with the alphabetical listings, where he appears between 1870 and 1879.

Directory entries:
Wright 1870–1879 NC, 1871–1875 P

Ring, John
Ring, John, & Co.
Ring, Ann Morley
22 Redcliff Street (1808–1813); 16 Redcliff Street (1812–1813); 46 Redcliff Street (1818); 20 Temple Street (1820); 15 Bath Street (1819–1840)

John Ring is listed with a china, glass and Staffordshire warehouse at 22 Redcliff Street in 1808 Mathews and 1809 Holden, and the same business is listed by Mathews from 1809 to 1813 in the style of John Ring & Co. Additional premises at 16 Redcliff Street are listed in 1812 and 1813. John Ring is also listed as an individual at 22 Redcliff Street in 1812 and 1813, and at Hillsbridge Place from 1814 to 1817. Further entries for John Ring appear in 1818 Mathews and 1818 Evans, still with a china, glass and Staffordshire warehouse, but at 46 Redcliff Street.

John Ring was presumably succeeded by his wife, Ann Morley Ring, since she is listed as a "dealer in china, glass, and Staffordshire ware, wholesale and retail" in the Mathews directories from 1819, trading at 15 Bath Street. She continued until 1840, although the earthenware business declined and in the later years she is listed only as a grocer and tea dealer. One unexplained entry for John Ring appears in 1820 Mathews, where he is listed as a Staffordshire ware dealer at 20 Temple Street.

Directory entries:
Mathews 1808–1840 NC
1809 Holden NC 1811 Holden NC 1818 Evans GCED

Ring, John, & Co.
Ring & Cookworthy
Ring, John
Temple Backs (1803–1815); Redcliff Back (1816–1818)

John Ring & Co. are listed as Tobacco pipe manufacturers at Temple Backs in the Mathews directories between 1803 and 1809. This business would appear to have been continued in the name of Ring & Cookworthy, listed as tobacco pipe manufacturers at Temple Backs from 1810 to 1815, and at Redcliff Back in 1816 and 1817. John Ring is also listed as a pipe manufacturer at Redcliff Back, along with his earthenware warehouse, in 1818 Mathews and 1818 Evans.

Directory entries:
Mathews 1803–1818 NC
1809 Holden NC 1816 Evans TPM 1818 Evans TPM
1811 Holden NC 1817 Evans TPM

Ring, Joseph
Ring, Taylor & Carter
Ring & Carter
Temple Backs

Joseph Ring operated the Bristol Pottery in Water Lane, Temple Backs, and is listed as the "only manufacturer of Queen's ware" in Bailey's directory of 1787. He died in 1788 and was succeeded by Ring, Taylor & Carter who are listed as potters in 1792 Universal only. They were in turn succeeded by Ring & Carter, again listed as the "only manufacturers of Queen's ware" in the Mathews directories from 1793 to 1797. A retail warehouse at Bath Street is mentioned in 1795 and 1797, the address given as 7 Bath Street in 1795.

Directory entries:
Mathews 1793–1797 NC

1787 Bailey NC	1792 Universal NC

Ring, Joseph II
Ring, Sarah
Water Lane (1797–1807); 14 Bath Street (1808–1817); 16 High Street (1818–1820)

Joseph Ring II, son of the Joseph Ring who was instrumental in the early years of the Bristol Pottery, held some interest in the concern after his father's death. He is listed as an individual at Water Lane in 1797 Mathews, and then as a potter at number 2 or 3 Water Lane between 1799 and 1807. In 1808 he is shown as proprietor of the china and glass warehouse at 14 Bath Street, which was also connected with the Bristol Pottery under Henry Carter & Co. (qv). From 1809 through to 1813 he is also listed as a manufacturer of earthenware, again reflecting his connection with the pottery, although Jacksons & Price state that he was not a partner until 1813 when the firm became Carter & Pountney. The china and glass warehouse at 14 Bath Street is still listed at this period, and Ring's residence is given as the Pottery in Temple Backs.

From 1814 Joseph Ring was succeeded by his wife, Sarah, listed with the warehouse, initially described as "china and glass warehouse, wholesale, retail, and for exportation", from 1814 to 1820. The address is listed as 14 Bath Street until 1817 and then 16 High Street, although this is listed as 13 High Street in 1818 Evans. She is also listed as a manufacturer of earthenware in 1814, and as a manufacturer of tobacco pipes in 1815 and 1816.

Directory entries:
Mathews 1797–1820 NC

1809 Holden NC	1816 Evans GCED	1817 Evans GCED
1811 Holden NC	1816 Evans TPM	1818 Evans GCED

Ring, Richard Frank, & Co.
Ring, Richard Frank
Spring Gardens, Avon Street, Great Gardens (1812–1830); Temple Back (1816–1848)

Richard Frank Ring & Co. are listed as tobacco pipe manufacturers at Great Gardens in the Mathews directories from 1812 to 1830, although there is no entry in 1815. In the first three years the entries ask for orders to be left at the Bristol Pottery (1812–1813), or at 14 Bath Street (1814) which was also related to the Pottery. From 1816 the firm is described as "Ohio" tobacco pipe manufacturers. During this period Richard Frank Ring was also a coal merchant, listed at at the Pottery Coal Wharf, Temple Back, from 1816.

Elizabeth Ring & Co.
Earthenware, China, Glass, &c.
from the first Manufacturers.

Services of Earthenware, China & Gla
to pattern, also of the newly invente
Stone China, Lustres, Girandoles.
Lamps. &c. &c. &c.

Elizabeth Ring & Co. *An advertisement, engraved by Burnell, showing the shop front at 8 High Street. This appeared in the Mathews directory of 1834. (BMAG)*

From 1831 the two businesses were combined at the Temple Back address under the style of Richard Frank Ring trading alone. He was succeeded by Ring & Son (listed 1849–1861), Charles Ring & Co. (1862–1863), and Richard Charles Ring & Co. (1864–1885). The tobacco pipe business is last mentioned in 1883.

Directory entries:
Mathews 1812–1814 NC, 1816–1885 NC

1816 Evans TPM	1817 Evans TPM	1818 Evans TPM
1817 Evans NC	1818 Evans NC	

Ring, Robert & Thomas
Ring, Robert
Ring, Robert jun.
Ring, Robert M.

Thomas Street (1803–1811); Water Lane, Temple Backs (1812–1848)

Robert & Thomas Ring are listed as coopers and lime burners at Thomas Street in the Mathews directories between 1803 and 1811. From 1812 Robert Ring is listed alone as a lime burner only at Water Lane, Temple Back, with his residence shown as 5 Guinea Street (1812–1814) and later Durbin Cottage, Back Lane, Bedminster (from 1821). He was succeeded by Robert Ring junior (listed 1830–1836), and Robert M. Ring (1837–1848).

Directory entries:
Mathews 1803–1848 NC

1817 Evans NC	1818 Evans NC

Roberts, Mary

Fishponds

Mary Roberts is classified as an earthenware manufacturer at Fishponds in 1868 Slater, although she is described as a general dealer and not as a potter. She probably included some pottery in her trading, but is not listed in the Mathews or Wright directories of the period.

Directory entries:
1868 Slater EM

S

Serle, Samuel

Avon Street, St Philip's

Samuel Serle is listed as a red ware potter and classified as a brown ware potter at Avon Street only in 1828 Mathews.

Directory entries:
Mathews 1828 NC, 1828 PB

Sheppard, Samuel
Sheppard, Mary

Bread Street (1801); Avon Street, St Philip's (1803–1827)

Samuel Sheppard is listed in the Mathews directories from 1801 to 1823, initially at Bread Street but then at Avon Street, St Philip's. The earlier entries describe him as a manufacturer of red and glazed ware, specifically chimney and garden pots, but later he is noted simply as a brown ware potter. He was succeeded by Mary Sheppard, presumably his widow, who once again is listed as a brown ware potter at Avon Street in the Mathews directories between 1824 and 1827. She is mostly listed simply as Mrs. Sheppard. The entries for Samuel in 1822 Pigot and for Mary in 1824 Pigot are both in the classification for potters but note also bricks and tiles. The Sheppards were succeeded by Jonathan Flood (qv).

Directory entries:
Mathews 1801–1827 NC, 1820–1821 PB, 1823–1827 PB

1809 Holden NC	1816 Evans P	1818 Evans PS	1824 Pigot P
1811 Holden NC	1817 Evans PS	1822 Pigot P	

Skidmore, Richard

Thomas Street (1792); St Philip's (1795); Temple Backs (1801–1803)

Richard Skidmore is listed as a potter at Thomas Street in 1792 Universal, a pot-maker at St Philip's in 1795 Mathews, and a pot-maker for glass houses at Temple Backs in 1801 and 1803 Mathews. He is also listed as a maltster in 1793 and 1795. Other entries between 1797 and 1808 list a Richard Skidmore as a gentleman at St Philip's, but these are probably not related to the potter.

Directory entries:
Mathews 1793–1808 NC
1792 Universal NC

Smith, Isaac

Orchard Street, Horton Street

Isaac Smith is classified as a potter at Orchard Street, Horton Street, in 1856 Kelly although the alphabetical list shows him as a dealer in brown ware and not a manufacturer. He does not appear in the Mathews directories of the period.

Directory entries:
1856 Kelly P

Spokes & Bourne

Avon Street, St Philip's

Spokes & Bourne are classified as potters at Avon Street, St Philip's, in 1816 Evans, and are listed as making stone ware pottery in the Mathews directory of the same year. They may have succeeded Cole & Spokes (qv) and were in turn succeeded by John Spokes (qv).

Directory entries:
Mathews 1816 NC
1816 Evans P

Spokes, James

Avon Street, St Philip's

James Spokes is classified as a stone ware potter at Avon Street, St Philip's, in the Evans directories of 1817 and 1818, but these entries could well be misprints for John Spokes (qv).

Directory entries:
1817 Evans PS 1818 Evans PS

Spokes, John
Spokes, Samuel
Spokes, John jun. (or J.D.)
Spokes, John T.
Spokes, Sarah
Spokes, John Thomas
Avon Street, St Philip's

John Spokes succeeded Spokes & Bourne (qv) and is listed as a stoneware potter at Avon Street, St Philip's, in the Mathews directories and elsewhere between 1817 and 1838 (although no entry appears in 1819). There are no entries for the Spokes family between 1839 and 1843, but thereafter the business continued until about 1887. There is considerable confusion over the exact sequence, largely caused by the family's use of the name John for every generation. According to the Mathews and Wright alphabetical listings, the sequence was Samuel Spokes (listed 1844–1848), John Spokes junior (1847 and 1849–1857), John T. Spokes (1858–1864), Sarah Spokes (1865–1869), and John Thomas Spokes (1872–1887). Thereafter, although J. Spokes is still listed as an earthenware manufacturer in 1888 and as an earthenware dealer in 1889 Bennett, John Thomas Spokes is shown as an individual with no trade given at Primrose Villa, Eastville, in the Wright directories until 1896. Other directories tend to agree with this sequence but the dates vary slightly and John Spokes junior sometimes appears as J.D. Spokes.

The earlier entries describe the products as brown and stoneware, but later references are to brown ware or red ware, and from about 1870 only redware is mentioned. The address is given as Avon Street, St Philip's, throughout, although a second address at Barton Hill is listed in 1870 Kelly and 1872 Morris.

Directory entries:
Mathews 1817–1818 NC, 1820–1838 NC, 1844–1869 NC, 1823–1838 PS, 1844–1862 PS, 1863–1869 PB
Wright 1872–1896 NC, 1870 P, 1872–1887 P

1822 Pigot P	1852 Scammell PS	1869 Bristol NC	1883 Kelly P
1824 Pigot P	1853 Scammell PS	1870 Kelly P	1885 Kelly P
1830 Pigot P	1858 Slater EM	1872 Morris PSM	1888 Bennett EM
1846 Slater P	1859 Harrison BSW	1875 Kelly P	1889 Bennett ED
1848 Hunt PS	1865 Webster EM	1876 Morris PSM	
1850 Hunt PS	1866 Harrod EM	1879 Kelly P	
1850 Slater EM	1868 Slater EM	1880 Slater EM	

T

Taylor, William
10 Water Lane

William Taylor is listed as a potter at 10 Water Lane in 1775 Sketchley.

Directory entries:
1775 Sketchley NC

Tripp & Co.
Thomas Street

Tripp & Co. are listed as brown stone potters at Thomas Street in the Mathews directories of 1808 and 1809 and in the Holden directories of 1809 and 1811.

Directory entries:
Mathews 1808–1809 NC
1809 Holden NC 1811 Holden NC

Tuckett, Alfred, & Co.
Temple Meads; Shirehampton

Alfred Tuckett & Co. are classified as stoneware manufacturers in 1861 Kelly. Their address is given as Temple Meads, with works at Shirehampton, and they are described as "manufacturers of glazed stoneware sewage pipes, draining pipes, bricks, tiles &c." There is no mention of the firm in other directories, although Alfred Tuckett is listed as an individual in the Mathews directories, his address given as Shirehampton or Myrtle Hall, Shirehampton, between 1856 and 1872.

Directory entries:
Mathews 1856–1872 NC
1861 Kelly SM

JOSEPH RING,
Succeſſor to *Richard Frank* in the Pottery Buſineſs,
CONTINUES the MANUFACTORY of
The BRISTOL STONE WARE,
And ſells all Sorts of *Queen's and other Ware*,
WHOLESALE and RETAIL.

Prices of Stone Ware at Twelve Months Credit:

1 Gallon Bottles - per Hundred
2 Gallon ditto - ditto.
Full 10 Quart ditto - ditto.
Full 3 Gallon ditto - ditto.

PICKLING POTS and OTHER GOODS proportionably low.

Facsimile of Joseph Ring's first card.

Joseph Ring. *A facsimile of Joseph Ring's first trade card, noting his succession to Richard Frank but concentrating on stoneware. This card must predate Ring's decision to manufacture Queen's Ware (or creamware) at the Bristol Pottery. (BMAG)*

V

Victoria Pottery Co. Ltd.

Victoria Pottery, St Philip's Marsh

The Victoria Pottery Co. Ltd. succeeded John Ellis at the Victoria Pottery, St Phillip's Marsh, and is listed in the Mathews and Wright directories between 1866 and 1874. An office at the Royal Insurance Buildings in Corn Street is also listed in 1866 and 1867. The address is given as Avon Bank in 1868 Slater which also lists John Ellis as the managing director. The company name is sometimes given as the Bristol Victoria Pottery Co. Ltd. (in 1870 Kelly for example), and the entries for Ellis & Co. Ltd. which appear in 1866 Kelly and 1867 Morris almost certainly relate to this company.

Directory entries:

Mathews 1866–1869 NC, 1866–1869 P
Wright 1870–1874 NC, 1870–1873 P

1866 Kelly P	1868 Slater EM	1870 Kelly P
1867 Morris P	1869 Bristol NC	

Walker, W.W.
Walker, W.W., & Co.

Thomas Street

W.W. Walker is listed in the Mathews directories at Thomas Street between 1808 and 1815, and also in 1816 Evans. No trade is given in 1808 and 1809, and from 1810 to 1813 the listing is for W.W. Walker & Co., described as brown stone potters. Thereafter Walker is listed alone, still described as a brown stone potter.

Directory entries:

Mathews 1808–1815 NC
1816 Evans P

Walton, Gooddy & Cripps
Walton, Gooddy & Cripps Ltd.

Canon's Marsh

Walton, Gooddy & Cripps succeeded Gooddy, Cripps & Sons Ltd. at Canon's Marsh and are classified as potters in the Wright directories from 1901 to 1904. Once again, they were dealers and not manufacturers, described in the alphabetical lists as marble merchants. The style is given as a limited company from 1902 and they continued in business until at least 1906.

Directory entries:

Wright 1901–1906 NC, 1901–1904 P

Webb, Charles
Webb, W.
Webb, Leah

Temple Back

Charles Webb succeeded Jonathan Flood at Temple Back and is listed as a red ware and water pipe manufacturer in the Mathews directories between 1848 and 1852. He was also an apothecary and chemist, listed at 2 Temple Street in the Hunt directories of 1848 and 1850, and also in 1850 Slater. He was succeeded by Mrs. Leah Webb, presumably his widow, who is listed between 1853 and 1860. An entry for W. Webb (late Flood) in 1853 Scammell may simply be a misprint for Leah Webb. The firm's products included draining pipes and chimney pots, listed from 1851, and garden pots, from 1856.

Directory entries:

Mathews 1848–1860 NC, 1848–1860 PB

1848 Hunt PS	1852 Scammell PS	1857 Slater EM
1850 Hunt PS	1853 Scammell PS	1858 Slater EM
1850 Slater EM	1856 Kelly P	1859 Harrison BSW

White, Frederick James

Ridgeway Lane, Fishponds

Frederick James White is listed as a red ware potter at Ridgeway Lane, Fishponds, in 1885 Kelly, but there appear to be no relevant entries in the Wright directories at this period. This is presumably the F.J. White who is mentioned by Pountney in connection with the White family businesses (see below). He states that White left Bristol with his son in 1893 to set up a stoneware manufactory at Denver, Colorado, and died there in December 1919.

Directory entries:

1885 Kelly P

White, Joseph
White, Joseph, & Sons
White & Doubting
White, William

Rich's Buildings, Redcross Street

Joseph White is listed as a tobacco pipe manufacturer at Rich's buildings, Redcross Street, in the Mathews directories between 1829 and 1845, although the firm is listed as Joseph White & Sons between 1838 and 1841. The early entries, until 1837, also mention a china and Staffordshire warehouse. He is also classified as a stoneware potter from 1842 to 1846, the entries listing yellow ware and black Egyptian, and this side of the business appears to have been in succession to White & Doubting, who are listed making yellow ware and black teapots in 1840, and classified as stoneware potters, again making yellow ware and black Egyptian, in 1840 and 1841.

The Staffordshire warehouse appears to have been continued by another relation, William White, listed between 1841 and 1851. He was also involved in the manufacture of black and Rockingham teapots and his products included stone jugs from 1842 and fire clay chimney pots from 1843. He appears to have continued Joseph White's tobacco pipe business from 1846 and the manufacture of yellow ware and black Egyptian from 1847. The final mention of William White appears in 1852 Scammell.

Directory entries:

Mathews 1829–1851 NC, 1840–1851 PS

1842 Pigot P	1848 Hunt PS	1850 Slater EM
1846 Slater P	1850 Hunt PS	1852 Scammell PS

White, Joseph jun. & James
White, James, Joseph & William
White, James & Joseph Augustus
White, Joseph Augustus

Rich's Buildings, Redcross Street (until 1839); Millpond Street, Baptist Mills (from 1839)

The White brothers, Joseph junior and James, were the sons of the Joseph White who manufactured tobacco pipes (see above). They started potting at the family establishment of Rich's Buildings, Redcross Street, where they are described as potters for yellow ware in 1829 Mathews. They are listed at Redcross Street until 1839, about the time that Pountney states they had a dispute with their father, but thereafter their business is shown at Baptist Mills, first listed in 1839 Robson. Entries continue in the Mathews directories until 1855 and products mentioned include black teapots (from 1839), and Egyptian black and Rockingham teapots together with stone jugs from 1842. Other products included gold lustre ware (mentioned from 1842 to 1846), tobacco pipes (1847 to 1853), and toy wares (1848 Hunt, 1850 Hunt, and 1850 Slater). The last alphabetical entry for the brothers appears in the Mathews directory for 1855, although classified entries continue until 1863.

Pountney states that the brothers retired in 1855, leaving the business to their sons, but this period is extremely confusing in the directories. It would appear that the succession was James, Joseph & William White (listed 1856 to 1860), followed by James & Joseph Augustus White (listed 1861 to 1891), although Joseph Augustus White is listed alone in the Wright directories between 1870 and 1880. James is listed as James junior in 1864 Mathews. Pountney notes that the last surviving partner died in 1875 and that the business was carried on by executors, and this may explain the inconsistencies in the styles used in the directories. Generally the firms are listed simply as manufacturers of pottery and earthenware, or just potters, although the entry in 1861 Kelly mentions refined tobacco pipes and terra cotta. This is the only directory to name the pottery itself, which is listed as the Phoenix Pottery. The final entry appears in 1891, and the firm appears to have been succeeded by the Yate Pottery Ltd. (qv).

Members of the White family who were partners in the firm are occasionally listed individually with their residences. These include James White of Frome Villa, Lower Ashley Road in 1859 Harrison and 1867 Morris, Joseph Augustus White of 15 Cornwallis Place, Baptist Mills, in 1859 Harrison and 1861 Kelly, and Joseph White of Landfield Villa, Stapleton Road, in 1867 Morris.

Directory entries:
Mathews 1829–1869 NC, 1829–1859 PS, 1860–1869 PB
Wright 1870–1891 NC, 1870–1891 P

1830 Pigot P	1856 Kelly P	1866 Kelly P	1880 Slater EM
1839 Robson P	1857 Slater EM	1867 Morris P	1883 Kelly P
1842 Pigot P	1858 Slater EM	1868 Slater EM	1885 Kelly P
1846 Slater P	1859 Harrison BSW	1869 Bristol NC	1888 Bennett EM
1848 Hunt PS	1859 Harrison EM	1870 Kelly P	1889 Bennett ED
1850 Hunt PS	1861 Kelly P	1872 Morris PSM	1889 Kelly P
1850 Slater EM	1863 Kelly P	1875 Kelly P	
1852 Scammell PS	1865 Webster EM	1876 Morris PSM	
1853 Scammell PS	1866 Harrod EM	1879 Kelly P	

Ring & Carter. *A trade card by an engraver named Doddrell showing a thrower with his young helpers, surrounded by examples of creamware shapes typical of the period. (BMAG)*

Joseph Ring II. *A decorative illustrated trade card by an engraver named Johnson of John Street, Bristol.* *(BMAG)*

White's Yate Pottery Ltd.
See: Yate Pottery Ltd.

Whitehead, Isaac
Avon Street
Isaac Whitehead is listed at Avon Street as a potter in 1785 Browne, and also as a red potter in 1787 Bailey.
Directory entries:
1785 Browne NC 1787 Bailey NC

Wilcox, Cook & Co.
St Philip's
Wilcox, Cook & Co. are listed at St Philip's in 1816 Mathews, where they are described as stoneware and tobacco-pipe manufacturers, and also in the classifications for potters and tobacco-pipe manufacturers in 1816 Evans.
Directory entries:
Mathews 1816 NC
1816 Evans P 1816 Evans TPM

Wilcox, J.H.
St Philip's
J.H. Wilcox is classified as a stoneware potter at St Philip's in the Evans directories for 1817 and 1818, but does not appear in the Mathews directories of the period. The entries appear to relate to John H. Wilcox, Esq. of Hambrook, presumably succeeding Wilcox, Cook & Co. (qv).
Directory entries:
1817 Evans PS 1818 Evans PS

Wild, John
Hillgrove Street (1809–1811); 66 Broad Mead (1812); 1 Horse Fair (1816–1828)
John Wild was not a potter but is listed as a "china and glass gilder, enameller, &c." in the Mathews directories at Hillgrove Street from 1809 to 1811, and at 66 Broad Mead in 1812. He reappears as a glass stainer at 1 Horse Fair in 1818, although he is also listed as a china mender, glass and china dealer, or glass stainer in the Evans directories from 1816. He continued at Horse Fair until succeeded by Mrs. Wild, presumably his widow, who is listed from 1829, and then by A. & J. Wild, listed from 1834, and finally J. Wild, listed from 1846 to 1849.
The business seems to have concentrated on glass in the later years, the last mention as china enamellers and menders appearing in 1839. The surname is given as Wylde in two of the entries in 1818 Evans.
Directory entries:
Mathews 1809–1812 NC, 1818–1849 NC
1816 Evans CMend 1817 Evans CMend 1818 Evans CMend 1818 Evans GCED
1816 Evans GCED 1817 Evans GCED 1818 Evans GStain

Wildgoose, Frederick
Easton Road (1852–1853); Stapleton Road (1854–1868); St Philip's Marsh (1862–1868)

Frederick Wildgoose is classified as a brown ware potter in the Mathews directories between 1857 and 1868, although the alphabetical entries show that he started as a brick and tile maker at 3 Easton Buildings, Easton Road, in 1852. He had moved to 16 Victoria Place in Stapleton Road by 1854, and again to 3 Regina Place, still in Stapleton Road, by 1855. He continued to produce bricks and tiles, but brown ware pottery is first noted in 1857 and red ware from 1858. An address in St Philip's Marsh was added from 1862. He apparently ceased trading about 1868, although he is still listed as a private individual at the Regina Place address until 1872.

Directory entries:
Mathews 1852–1863 NC, 1865–1872 NC, 1857–1868 PB
Wright 1870–1872 NC
1869 Bristol NC

Woodville Pottery Co.
Lion Chambers, Broad Street

The Woodville Pottery Co. is listed in the classification for potters in the Wright directories of 1896 and 1897, where the address is shown as Lion Chambers, Brood (sic) Street, with I. Oppenheim as their agent. Israel Oppenheim is himself listed as a manufacturer's agent at 2 Lion Chambers, Broad Street, from 1894 until at least 1906, with his residence at 12 Woodstock Avenue, Redland, from 1897 to 1900. The pottery company was not based in Bristol.

Directory entries:
Wright 1894–1906 NC, 1896–1897 P

Yabbicom, Henry & Thomas
Yabbicom, H. & E.
Avon Street, St Philip's

H. & T. Yabbicom are first listed as manufacturers of crucibles and brown stone ware at Avon Street, St Philip's, in 1812 Mathews. Similar entries continue until 1832 although there is no further mention of crucibles, and from 1824 they are also described as manufacturers of improved water pipes. The only directory to give their full names is 1830 Pigot which lists them as Henry & Thomas Yabbicomb. The listing of their initials as H. & F. in 1822 Pigot is probably a printer's error. They were succeeded by H. & E. Yabbicom, listed by Mathews from 1833 to 1842 (although the classified lists still give H. & T. Yabbicom until 1837). From 1837 the description includes pantiles and fire bricks in addition to the stone ware and water pipes. In 1839 Robson the entries also mention sugar moulds and a second address at Pipe Lane, Temple, but this would appear to be an error for Henry Yabbicom (qv). In some directories the surname is listed as Yabbicomb or even as Yabbicome.

Directory entries:
Mathews 1812–1842 NC, 1820–1821 PS, 1823–1837 PS

1816 Evans P	1818 Evans PB	1824 Pigot P	1839 Robson P
1817 Evans PB	1822 Pigot P	1830 Pigot P	1839 Robson SW

Yabbicom & Son
Yabbicom, Henry

Westbury (1795); St Philip's (1797–1842); Temple Backs (1806–1862)

Yabbicom & Son are listed as sugar, chimney, and garden pot manufacturers in the Mathews directories between 1795 and 1809. Their address is given as Westbury in 1795, Avon Street, St Philip's, between 1797 and 1799 (with a residence still at Westbury for 1797 and 1798), Cheese Lane, St Philip's, from 1801 to 1805, and St Philip's and Temple Backs from 1806. Henry Yabbicom appears as an individual at 1 Redcross Street in the Mathews directories between 1805 and 1809, but from 1810 he succeeded Yabbicom & Son. The St Philip's address is not mentioned in any directories after 1842, and the Temple Back address is shown as Pipe Lane in most non-Mathews directories from 1850. He is listed by Mathews and others until 1862.

In the early entries Yabbicom is shown as a manufacturer of sugar, chimney and garden pots, but the lists of products include pantiles and fire-bricks from 1837, and improved water pipes from 1843. From about 1854 he is shown simply as a manufacturer of brown stoneware, although drain tiles are sometimes also mentioned. His residence is given as St Philip's Place (1812–1835), St Philip's Plain (1836–1842), Broad Plain (1843–1845), and 23 King Square (1846–1854). There are many variants of the surname, including Yabbicorn and Yabbicombe, but Yabbicomb is the most common, appearing in several of the earlier directories, and fairly consistently in the Mathews directories from 1849 onwards.

Directory entries:

Mathews 1795–1862 NC, 1820–1821 PB, 1823–1841 PB, 1842–1862 PS

1809 Holden NC	1822 Pigot P	1848 Hunt PS	1856 Kelly P
1811 Holden NC	1824 Pigot P	1850 Hunt PS	1857 Slater EM
1816 Evans P	1830 Pigot P	1850 Slater EM	1858 Slater EM
1817 Evans PS	1842 Pigot P	1852 Scammell PS	1861 Kelly EM
1818 Evans PS	1846 Slater P	1853 Scammell PS	

Yate Pottery Ltd.
Yate Fire-Clay & Brick Co. Ltd.

40 Broad Street

The Yate Pottery Ltd. is listed with offices at 40 Broad Street in the Wright directories between 1892 and 1897. The firm appears to have succeeded J. & J. White, and for the first two years the entries list the firm as White's Yate Pottery Ltd. They were succeeded by the Yate Fire-Clay & Brick Co. Ltd. who are listed from 1898 to 1902.

Directory entries:

Wright 1892–1902 NC, 1892–1897 P

1899 Town P	1900 Town P	1901 Town P

Appendix

Bristol Directories and their Publishers

The directories listed in the sections below include all those known to cover Bristol and to include relevant information about potters. The publishers are listed alphabetically with a short description followed by a list of all their relevant directories. In each case the full title is quoted, with the date of publication and, where possible, any additional dating information contained in the directory itself. More detailed information is considered unnecessary here, but cross references are provided to the bibliographical lists by Norton and Shaw & Tipper which are invaluable guides to surviving directories. It must, however, be noted that both volumes have been found to suffer from a few inaccuracies and omissions, and these are noted where they are felt to be relevant to this survey.

William Bailey

Birmingham (1783), London (1784)

William Bailey was the first person to make a serious attempt at producing a national directory. His first venture was a Northern Directory published in 1781, followed by a Western and Midland Directory, published in 1783. This was in turn followed by a British Directory in four volumes, published during 1784. The 1783 and 1784 directories both include Bristol, and while the contents are not identical, it is probable that they were based on the same survey, and the potters included are certainly unchanged. Bailey subsequently published a local directory of Bristol and Bath, originally intended to be part of a larger series, in 1787. Bailey's directories are not classified.

1783 Bailey. *Bailey's Western and Midland Directory, or Merchant's and Tradesman's Useful Companion, for the Year 1783* (Norton 2). Dedication and Advertisement not dated.

1784 Bailey. *Bailey's British Directory, or Merchant's and Trader's Useful Companion, for the Year 1784, in Four Volumes. Volume the Second. The Western Directory, The First Edition* (Norton 3). Dedication in Volume 1 is dated 4 June 1784, and refers to the publication of Volume 2 'without fail, the beginning of July'.

1787 Bailey. *The Bristol and Bath Directory . . . 1787* (Norton 253). Dedication not dated.

Peter Barfoot & John Wilkes

London

Peter Barfoot and John Wilkes were granted a Royal Patent in 1789 to produce a national directory, which appeared as *The Universal British Directory of Trade, Commerce, and Manufacture* in five volumes between 1790 and 1798. The directory was produced in parts and the earlier volumes were reprinted to make sets, usually with little or no correction. Volume 1 can be found dated 1790, 1791 and 1793, and the other volumes are all undated. Bristol appears as part 17 in Volume 2 and Norton quotes evidence that this section was published by 20 February 1792. The mayor is listed as John Noble, a merchant, who was in office from 29 September 1791 for twelve months. The author of the Bristol section was almost certainly John Reed (qv), since he issued offprint pages with a new title page and dedication as *The New Bristol Directory for the Year 1792*. The directory is not classified.

1792 Universal. *The Universal British Directory of Trade, Commerce, and Manufacture, Volume the Second* (Norton 18). Not dated.

Bennett & Co. Ltd.
Birmingham

Bennett & Co. published a string of business directories covering various English and Welsh counties between 1888 and 1936. Bristol appears in two editions with different combinations of counties dated 1888 and a third dated 1889. The relevant classifications are 'Bottle Manufacturers' and either 'Earthenware Manufacturers' (1888) or 'Earthenware Dealers', which includes manufacturers (1889).

1888 Bennett. *Bennett's Business Directory . . . 1888* (Shaw & Tipper 64 and Shaw & Tipper 136). Two different editions with the same information for Bristol.

1889 Bennett. *Bennett's Business Directory . . . 1889* (Not listed by Shaw & Tipper).

G. du Boistel & Co.
See: Sharp & Co.

Bristol Printing Co. Ltd.
Bristol

This firm published a single directory of Bristol in 1869. It is not classified and several firms do not appear in the alphabetical list.

1869 Bristol. *Bristol and Clifton Postal Directory . . . 1869* (Shaw & Tipper 471).

Arthur Browne & Son
Bristol

Sketchley's pioneering Bristol directory of 1775 was followed a decade later by a similar publication printed for Arthur Browne & Son and seven other individuals. The directory is not classified.

1785 Browne. *The Bristol Directory . . . 1785* (Norton 252). Advertisement not dated.

Browne & Manchee
See: John Evans & Co.

John Evans & Co.
Bristol

John Evans & Co. clearly intended to compete with the established Mathews directories, and issued classified directories in 1816 and 1817. A third and final edition appeared in 1818 under the same title, although it was printed and published by Browne & Manchee. Relevant classifications include 'China Enamellers', 'China Menders', 'Earthenware and China Manufacturers', 'Glass, China & Earthenware Dealers', 'Potters' (either Brown Ware or Stone Ware), and 'Tobacco Pipe Makers'.

1816 Evans. *The Bristol Index, or Evans's Directory, for the Year 1816* (Norton 313). Advertisement dated 18 April 1816.

1817 Evans. *The Bristol Index, or Evans's Directory, for the Year 1817* (Norton 314). Advertisement dated 7 January 1817.

1818 Evans. *The Bristol Index, or Evans's Directory, for the Year 1818* (Norton 315). Advertisement dated 20 January 1818.

Harrison, Harrod & Co.
London

Harrison, Harrod & Co. began publishing a series of directories in 1859, the first of which was the only one to cover Bristol. They were succeeded in 1861 by J.G.

Harrod & Co. (see below). The relevant classifications are 'Brown and Stone Warehouse Potters' and 'Earthenware Manufacturers'.

1859 Harrison. *Harrison, Harrod, & Co.'s Bristol Post-Office Directory and Gazetteer, with the Counties of Gloucestershire and Somersetshire . . . 1859* (Shaw & Tipper 117). Preface dated 1 January 1859.

J.G. Harrod & Co.

London and Norwich

J.G. Harrod & Co. succeeded Harrison, Harrod & Co. (see above) in 1861 and continued to produce a series of directories covering various counties until 1880. The only volume to cover Bristol appeared in 1866, although close examination suggests that it is only a reprint of Webster & Co.'s directory of the previous year. The two firms occupied neighbouring addresses in London and there may have been some collaboration between them. The relevant classifications are 'Earthenware Manufacturers' and 'Stoneware Manufacturers'.

1866 Harrod. *J.G. Harrod and Co.'s Post-Office Directory of Bristol, Glamorganshire, and Monmouthshire . . . 1866* (Shaw & Tipper 45). Preface dated 1866.

William Holden

London

William Holden began publishing a series of directories in 1799, originally covering only London. The fourth edition of 1805 incorporated some eighty-four other towns, including Bristol. This directory was reprinted, unchanged except for the title page, in 1808, but a new updated edition appeared in 1809. Bristol also appeared in one further Holden directory of 1811. Holden was succeeded by Thomas Underhill who continued to produce similar directories but none are relevant to this survey. Holden's directories are not classified.

1805 Holden. *Holden's Triennial Directory, Fourth Edition, for 1805, 1806, 1807. Second Volume . . . 1805* (Norton 21). The Address in Volume 1 includes a note that the Addenda 'will be published in April, 1805'.

1808 Holden. *Holden's Triennial Directory, Fourth Edition, Including the Year 1808* (Norton 22). This is purely a reprint of 1805 Holden with a new title page.

1809 Holden. *Holden's Triennial Directory, Fifth Edition, for 1809, 1810, 1811. Second Volume* (Norton 23). Address not dated.

1811 Holden. *Holden's Annual London and Country Directory, of the United Kingdom and Wales, in Three Volumes, for the Year 1811. Second Volume . . . 1811* (Norton 24). Advertisement in Volume 1 refers to 'the lateness in the year of the production'.

E. Hunt & Co.

London

E. Hunt & Co. published a confusing series of directories, mainly of western England and Welsh counties, between 1846 and 1852. Several editions were produced by binding together sections covering different areas. Bristol was included in at least ten editions issued between 1848 and 1851, and despite a comment to the contrary by Norton, was surveyed twice. The results of the first survey were printed in editions dated 1848 and 1849, after which the information was updated in time for editions dated 1850 and 1851. The contents vary, but where classified sections are included the relevant classification is 'Potters — Stone Ware'.

1848 Hunt. *Hunt & Co.'s City of Bristol, Clifton and Hotwells Directory, including [Ashton to*

Stapleton] . . . *January 1848* (Norton 316). Also *Hunt & Co.'s City of Bristol, Newport & Welch Towns Directory, including [Bristol to Swansea]* . . . *January 1848* (Norton 863). Address dated January 1848. Also *Hunt & Co.'s Directory & Topography for the Cities of Exeter and Bristol, and the Towns of [Bridgewater to Wellington]* . . . *1848* (Norton 173). Address dated 1848. Also *Hunt & Co.'s Directory & Court Guide for the Cities of Bath, Bristol, & Wells, and the Towns of [Bradford to Westbury]* . . . *May 1848* (Norton 760). Address dated May 1848.
1849 Hunt. *Hunt & Co.'s Directory & Topography for the Cities of Gloucester & Bristol, and the towns of [Berkeley to Wotton-under-Edge] with [Aberavon to Swansea]* . . . *March 1849* (Norton 250). Address dated March 1849. Also *Hunt & Co.'s Directory & Topography for the Cities of Gloucester & Bristol, and the towns of [Aberayron to Usk] with [Aberavon to Swansea]* . . . *June 1849* (Norton 864). Address dated June 1849. Also *Hunt & Co.'s Directory & Topography for the Cities of Gloucester & Bristol, and the Towns of [Carmarthen to St. Clears] with [Aberavon to Swansea]* . . . *July 1849* (Norton 865). Address dated July 1849.
1850 Hunt. *Hunt & Co.'s Directory & Topography for the City of Bristol, Bedminster, Clifton, Hotwells, and [Suburban Villages], also the Towns of [Axbridge to Weston] with [Banwell to Stanton-Drewe]* . . . *1850* (Shaw & Tipper 459). Address dated January 1850. Also *Hunt & Co.'s Directory & Topography for the City of Bristol, and the Towns of [Axbridge to Weston], also the Welsh Towns of [Cardigan to Tenby]* . . . *1850* (Norton 867). Address dated January 1850. Also *Hunt & Co.'s Directory & Topography of the Towns of [Axbridge to Yeovil]* . . . *to which is added a Descriptive Account of the City of Bristol* . . . *1850* (Norton 622, Shaw & Tipper 1200). Address dated July 1850.
1851 Hunt. *Hunt & Co.'s Directory of Dorsetshire, with part of Hants and Wilts [including the City of Salisbury, and Christchurch to Wilton], also of the City of Bristol, and the Towns of [Axbridge to Yeovil]* . . . *1851* (Norton 230). Address dated 1851.

Kelly & Co.
London

The famous directory publishing firm of Kelly's had its origins in 1835 or 1836 when Frederick Kelly, an inspector in the Post Office, purchased the rights to *The Post Office London Directory*. In 1845 the firm branched out and issued the first of a series of directories which by 1871 covered all English counties. The organisation went on to become by far the most important publisher of British directories. The imprint was originally W. Kelly & Co. but the initial was dropped by 1852 and the firm became a limited company by 1891. By 1897 the style was Kelly's Directories Ltd.

Bristol was first covered in an 1856 volume with Bath and Gloucestershire, and thereafter it was reissued approximately every four years. Apart from the first edition of 1856, the Bristol pages were a separate section, sometimes issued as a separate directory, but usually bound up with other counties, particularly Somerset or Gloucestershire. Various combinations are known and most are listed below but more are listed by Shaw & Tipper and others almost certainly exist, although the Bristol pages are always identical for any given year.

From 1904 Kelly's took over responsibility for publishing Wright's annual Bristol directory and discontinued their own Bristol operation. Apart from preliminary pages the Bristol sections in subsequent Kelly's directories are reprints of the current Wright directory. Thus 1906 Kelly is identical to 1906 Wright, and while it is listed below for completeness, it has been omitted elsewhere in this work.

The relevant classifications vary but include 'Brown Ware Manufacturers', 'Earthenware Manufacturers', 'Potters', 'Stoneware Manufacturers' and 'Stone Jar Manufacturers'.
1856 Kelly. *Post Office Directory of Gloucestershire, with Bath and Bristol* . . . *1856* (Related to Shaw

& Tipper 10). Preface dated March 1856.
1861 Kelly. *Kelly's Post Office Directory of Somersetshire, with the City of Bristol . . . 1861* (Shaw & Tipper 1196). Preface dated November 1861.
1863 Kelly. *The Post Office Directory of Shropshire, Herefordshire, and Gloucestershire, with the City of Bristol . . . 1863* (Shaw & Tipper 10). Also *The Post Office Directory of the City of Bristol, for 1863* (Not listed by Shaw & Tipper). Prefaces dated May 1863.
1866 Kelly. *Post Office Directory of Somerset and Bristol . . . 1866* (Related to Shaw & Tipper 1196). Also *The Post Office Directory of Somerset and Devon, with Bristol . . . 1866* (Shaw & Tipper 15). Prefaces dated July 1866.
1870 Kelly. *The Post Office Directory of Shropshire, Herefordshire, and Gloucestershire, with the City of Bristol . . . 1870* (Shaw & Tipper 10). Preface dated June 1870.
1875 Kelly. *The Post Office Directory of Somerset and Devon with Bristol . . . 1875* (Related to Shaw & Tipper 15). No preface in the only copy located.
1879 Kelly. *The Post Office Directory of Shropshire, Herefordshire, and Gloucestershire, with the City of Bristol. . . 1879* (Shaw & Tipper 10). The only copy located was a rebound Bristol-only section with no title page or preface.
1883 Kelly. *Kelly's Directory of Somersetshire, with the City of Bristol . . . 1883* (Shaw & Tipper 1196). Preface dated July 1883.
1885 Kelly. *Kelly's Directory of the City of Bristol, Gloucestershire, Shropshire and Herefordshire . . . 1885* (Shaw & Tipper 10). Preface dated October 1885.
1889 Kelly. *Kelly's Directory of Somersetshire and Gloucestershire, with the City of Bristol . . . 1889* (Shaw & Tipper 21). Also *Kelly's Directory of Somersetshire, with the City of Bristol . . . 1889* (Related to Shaw & Tipper 1196). Also *Kelly's Directory of Gloucestershire, with the City of Bristol . . . 1889* (Not listed by Shaw & Tipper). Prefaces dated November 1889.
1891 Kelly. *Kelly's Directory of the City of Bristol and its Immediate Neighbourhood . . . 1891* (Shaw & Tipper 482). No preface.
1894 Kelly. *Kelly's Directory of Somersetshire and Gloucestershire, with the City of Bristol . . . 1894* (Shaw & Tipper 21). No copy with preface could be located.
1897 Kelly. *Kelly's Directory of the Counties of Somerset and Gloucester, with the City of Bristol . . . 1897* (Shaw & Tipper 21). Also *Kelly's Directory of Somerset and City of Bristol . . . 1897* (Related to Shaw & Tipper 1196). Prefaces dated October 1897.
1902 Kelly. *Kelly's Directory of the Counties of Somerset and Gloucester, with the City of Bristol . . . 1902* (Shaw & Tipper 21). Also *Kelly's Directory of the Counties of Somerset and Devon with the City of Bristol . . . 1902* (Related to Shaw & Tipper 15). Prefaces dated January 1902.
1906 Kelly. *Kelly's Directory of the Counties of Somerset and Gloucester, with the City of Bristol . . . 1906* (Shaw & Tipper 21). Preface dated January 1906.

The Mathews Family

Bristol

The Mathews family produced one of the most complete sets of directories for any city apart from London. The first edition was published by William Matthews in 1793, and he continued to issue a new edition every two years until 1803, with an extra edition in 1798. The family surname appears as Mathews from 1803 onwards. From 1805 William was succeeded by Edward Mathews who started to publish the directory annually. The imprint became Joseph Mathews in 1812, M. Mathews in 1834, M. Mathews & Son in 1835, Matthew Mathews in 1847, and William S. Mathews in 1863. The last edition appeared in 1869, after which the directory was taken over by J. Wright & Co. (qv). The early editions were not classified but a 'Commercial List' was introduced in 1820 including a classification for 'Potters' with sub-sections for 'Brown Ware Potters' and 'Stone Ware Potters'. This arrangement continued except for 1822 when no commercial list appeared.

1793 Matthews. *Matthews's New Bristol Directory for the Year 1793–4* (Norton 255). No preface.
1795 Matthews. *Matthews's New Bristol Directory for the Year 1795* (Norton 256). No preface.
1797 Matthews. *Matthews's New Bristol Directory for the Year 1797* (Norton 257). No preface.
1798 Matthews. *Matthews's Complete Bristol Directory for the Year 1798* (Norton 258). No preface.
1799 Matthews. *Matthews's Complete Bristol Directory for the Years 1799 & 1800* (Norton 259). No preface.
1801 Matthews. *Matthews's Complete Bristol Directory, Corrected to May 1801* (Norton 260). No preface.
1803 Mathews. *Mathews's Complete Bristol Directory, Continued to May 1803* (Norton 261). No preface.
1805 Mathews. *Mathews's Complete Bristol Directory, Continued to February 1805* (Norton 262). Address not dated.
1806 Mathews. *Mathews's Complete Bristol Directory, Continued to January 1806* (Norton 263). Address not dated.
1807 Mathews. *Mathews's Complete Bristol Directory, Continued to January 1807* (Norton 264). Address dated 31 January 1807.
1808 Mathews. *Mathews's Complete Bristol Directory, Continued to February 1808* (Norton 265). Address not dated.
1809 Mathews. *Mathews's Complete Bristol Directory, Continued to February 1809* (Norton 266). Address not dated.
1810 Mathews. *Mathews's Complete Bristol Directory, Corrected to February 1810* (Norton 267). Address not dated
1811 Mathews. *Mathews's Complete Bristol Directory, Continued to February 1810 with a Corrected Supplement to February 1811* (Norton 268). Address not dated. This edition is largely a reissue of 1810, with only minor updates and a list of additional names, none of which are potters.
1812 Mathews. *Mathews's Complete Bristol Directory, Corrected to February 1812* (Norton 269). Address not dated.
1813 Mathews. *Mathews's Annual Bristol Directory for the Year 1813* (Norton 270). Address dated 25 January 1813.
1814 Mathews. *Mathews's Annual Bristol Directory for the Year 1814* (Norton 271). Address not dated.
1815 Mathews. *Mathews's Annual Bristol Directory for the Year 1815* (Norton 272). Address not dated.
1816 Mathews. *Mathews's Annual Bristol Directory for the Year 1816* (Norton 273). Address not dated.
1817 Mathews. *Mathews's Annual Bristol Directory for the Year 1817* (Norton 274). Address dated 1 January 1817.
1818 Mathews. *Mathews's Annual Bristol Directory for the Year 1818* (Norton 275). Address dated 16 December 1817.
1819 Mathews. *Mathews's Annual Bristol Directory for the Year 1819* (Norton 276). Address not dated.
1820 Mathews. *Mathews's Annual Bristol Directory for the Year 1820* (Norton 277). Address dated 4 January 1820.
1821 Mathews. *Mathews's Annual Bristol Directory and Commercial List for the Year 1821* (Norton 278). Address dated 7 January 1821.
1822 Mathews. *Mathews's Annual Bristol Directory for the Year 1822* (Norton 279). Address dated 1 January 1822.
1823 Mathews. *Mathews's Annual Bristol Directory and Commercial List for the Year 1823* (Norton 280). Address dated 20 January 1823.
1824 Mathews. *Mathews's Annual Bristol Directory and Commercial List for the Year 1824* (Norton 281). Address dated 1 January 1824.
1825 Mathews. *Mathews's Annual Bristol Directory and Commercial List for the Year 1825* (Norton 282). Address dated 4 January 1825.

1826 Mathews. *Mathews's Annual Bristol Directory and Commercial List for the Year 1826* (Norton 283). Address dated 19 January 1826.
1827 Mathews. *Mathews's Annual Bristol Directory and Commercial List for the Year 1827* (Norton 284). Preface dated 4 January 1827.
1828 Mathews. *Mathews's Annual Bristol Directory and Commercial List for the Year 1828* (Norton 285). Address dated 27 December 1827.
1829 Mathews. *Mathews's Annual Bristol Directory and Commercial List for the Year 1829* (Norton 286). Title not confirmed. Address dated 14 January 1829.
1830 Mathews. *Mathews's Annual Bristol Directory and Commercial List for 1830* (Norton 287). Address dated 1 January 1830.
1831 Mathews. *Mathews's Annual Bristol Directory and Commercial List for 1831* (Norton 288). Address dated 12 January 1831.
1832 Mathews. *Mathews's Annual Bristol Directory and Commercial List for 1832* (Norton 289). Address not dated.
1833 Mathews. *Mathews's Annual Bristol Directory and Commercial List for 1833* (Norton 290). Address dated 23 December 1832.
1834 Mathews. *Mathews's Annual Bristol Directory and Commercial List for 1834* (Norton 291). Address dated 1 January 1834.
1835 Mathews. *Mathewses' Annual Bristol Directory and Commercial List for 1835* (Norton 292). Address not dated.
1836 Mathews. *Mathews's Annual Bristol Directory and Commercial List for 1836* (Norton 293). Address dated 9 January 1836.
1837 Mathews. *Mathews's Annual Bristol Directory and Commercial List for the Year 1837* (Norton 294). Address dated 1 January 1837.
1838 Mathews. *Mathews's Annual Bristol Directory and Commercial List . . . 1838* (Norton 295). Advertisement dated 1 January 1838.
1839 Mathews. *Mathews's Annual Bristol Directory and Commercial List . . . 1839* (Norton 296). Address dated 1 January 1839.
1840 Mathews. *Mathews's Annual Bristol Directory and Almanack . . . 1840* (Norton 297). Address not dated.
1841 Mathews. *Mathews's Annual Bristol Directory and Almanack . . . 1841* (Norton 298). Address dated 1 January 1841.
1842 Mathews. *Mathews's Annual Bristol Directory and Almanack . . . 1842* (Norton 299). Address dated 1 January 1842.
1843 Mathews. *Mathews's Annual Bristol Directory and Almanack . . . 1843* (Norton 300). Address dated 1 January 1843.
1844 Mathews. *Mathews's Annual Bristol Directory and Almanack . . . 1844* (Norton 301). Address dated 1 January 1844.
1845 Mathews. *Mathews's Annual Bristol Directory and Almanack . . . 1845* (Norton 302). Address dated 1 January 1845.
1846 Mathews. *Mathews's Annual Bristol Directory and Almanack . . . 1846* (Norton 303). Address dated 1 January 1846.
1847 Mathews. *Mathews's Annual Bristol Directory and Almanack . . . 1847* (Norton 304). Address dated 1 January 1847.
1848 Mathews. *Mathews's Annual Bristol Directory and Almanack . . . 1848* (Norton 305). Address dated 1 January 1848.
1849 Mathews. *Mathews's Annual Bristol and Clifton Directory and Almanack . . . 1849* (Norton 306). Address not dated.
1850 Mathews. *Mathews's Annual Bristol and Clifton Directory and Almanack . . . 1850* (Norton 307, Shaw & Tipper 461). Address not dated.
1851 Mathews. *Mathews's Annual Bristol and Clifton Directory and Almanack . . . 1851* (Norton 308, Shaw & Tipper 461). Address not dated.
1852 Mathews. *Mathews's Annual Bristol and Clifton Directory and Almanack . . . 1852* (Norton

309, Shaw & Tipper 461). Address not dated.
1853 Mathews. *Mathews's Annual Bristol and Clifton Directory and Almanack . . . 1853* (Norton 310, Shaw & Tipper 461). Preface not dated.
1854 Mathews. *Mathews's Annual Bristol Directory and Almanack . . . 1854* (Norton 311, Shaw & Tipper 461). Preface dated 1 January 1854.
1855 Mathews. *Mathews's Annual Bristol Directory and Almanack . . . 1855* (Norton 312, Shaw & Tipper 461). Preface dated 1 January 1855.
1856 Mathews. *Mathews's Annual Bristol Directory and Almanack . . . 1856* (Shaw & Tipper 461). Preface not dated.
1857 Mathews. *Mathews's Annual Directory for the City and County of Bristol, including Clifton, Bedminster, and Surrounding Villages . . . 1857* (Shaw & Tipper 461). Address not dated.
1858 Mathews. *Mathews's Annual Directory for the City and County of Bristol, including Clifton, Bedminster, and Surrounding Villages . . . 1858* (Shaw & Tipper 466). Preface not dated.
1859 Mathews. *Mathews's Annual Directory for the City and County of Bristol, including Clifton, Bedminster, and Surrounding Villages . . . 1859* (Shaw & Tipper 466). No preface.
1860 Mathews. *Mathews's Annual Directory for the City and County of Bristol, including Clifton, Bedminster, and Surrounding Villages . . . 1860* (Shaw & Tipper 466). No preface.
1861 Mathews. *Mathews's Annual Directory for the City and County of Bristol, including Clifton, Bedminster, and Surrounding Villages . . . 1861* (Shaw & Tipper 466). No preface.
1862 Mathews. *Mathews's Annual Directory for the City and County of Bristol, including Clifton, Bedminster, and Surrounding Villages . . . 1862* (Shaw & Tipper 466). No preface.
1863 Mathews. *Mathews's Annual Directory for the City and County of Bristol, including Clifton, Bedminster, and Surrounding Villages . . . 1863* (Shaw & Tipper 466). Address dated January 1863.
1864 Mathews. *Mathews's Annual Directory for the City and County of Bristol, including Clifton, Bedminster, and Surrounding Villages . . . 1864* (Shaw & Tipper 466). Address not dated.
1865 Mathews. *Mathews's Annual Directory for the City & County of Bristol, including Clifton, Bedminster, and Surrounding Villages . . . 1865* (Shaw & Tipper 466). No preface.
1866 Mathews. *Mathews's Annual Directory for the City & County of Bristol, including Clifton, Bedminster, & Surrounding Villages . . . 1866* (Shaw & Tipper 466). No preface.
1867 Mathews. *Mathews's Annual Directory for the City & County of Bristol, including Clifton, Bedminster, and Surrounding Villages . . . 1867* (Shaw & Tipper 466). No preface.
1868 Mathews. *Mathews's Annual Directory for the City and County of Bristol, including Clifton, Bedminster, and Surrounding Villages . . . 1868* (Shaw & Tipper 466). No preface.
1869 Mathews. *Mathews's Annual Directory for the City and County of Bristol, including Clifton, Bedminster, and Surrounding Villages . . . 1869* (Shaw & Tipper 466). No preface.

Morris & Co.

Nottingham

Morris & Co. published a series of commercial directories covering various English counties between 1862 and 1880. Bristol was included in one directory of Somerset dated 1872 and two of Gloucestershire dated 1867 and 1876. Shaw & Tipper list a Gloucestershire edition for 1865 but the only copy extant is incomplete and actually appears to be an 1867 edition. The relevant classifications are 'Potters' and 'Stone Ware Manufacturers' (combined in 1872 and 1876).

1867 Morris. *Morris & Co.'s Commercial Directory and Gazetteer of Gloucestershire, with Bristol . . . 1867* (Shaw & Tipper 455). Preface dated April 1867.
1872 Morris. *Morris & Co.'s Commercial Directory and Gazetteer of Somersetshire, with Bristol . . . 1872* (Shaw & Tipper 1198). Preface dated August 1872.
1876 Morris. *Morris & Co.'s Commercial Directory & Gazetteer of Gloucestershire with Bristol and Monmouth. Second Edition . . . 1876* (Shaw & Tipper 455). Preface dated April 1876.

W.E. Owen & Co.
Leicester

W.E. Owen & Co. published a few directories covering various English and Welsh counties between 1877 and 1883. Bristol appears in two editions dated 1878 and one dated 1879, the information being the same in all three editions. The only relevant classification is 'Stone Ware Manufacturers'.

1878 Owen. *W.E. Owen & Co.'s General, Typographical, and Historical Directory for the Counties of Wiltshire, Somersetshire, with the Cities of Bristol and Bath . . . 1878* (Shaw & Tipper 134). No preface. Also *W.E. Owen & Co.'s General, Typographical, and Historical Directory for Glamorganshire, Monmouthshire, &c. . . . 1878* (Shaw & Tipper 1692). No preface. Also includes Somerset, Bristol and Bath, although they do not appear in the title.

1879 Owen. *W.E. Owen & Co.'s General, Typographical, and Historical Directory, for Gloucestershire, Wiltshire, Somersetshire, Monmouthshire, Radnorshire, with the Cities of Bristol and Bath . . . 1879* (Shaw & Tipper 61). No preface.

James Pigot & Co.
Manchester and London

James Pigot was arguably the greatest of the directory publishers in the first half of the nineteenth century. He published his first directory in 1811 and his first national directory followed in 1814. His operation expanded rapidly, and Norton classifies the earlier directories into five major surveys which were carried out between 1820 and 1853. Bristol was included in the Somerset survey of 1822, and the Gloucestershire surveys of 1830, 1842 and 1850. Norton suggests that another edition covering Gloucestershire may have been issued between 1830 and 1842 but no copy is known. Bristol was also included as a city in its own right in a Pigot directory of 1824.

Pigot himself died in 1843 and was succeeded by Isaac Slater (qv). The 1844 editions listed below were issued in Pigot's name but were actually the first to be published by Slater. Later editions are listed under Slater. Several different editions of each directory were produced, usually with different combinations of counties, and these can be confusing. All known editions are listed, but those which are simply reprints are noted as such and excluded from the list of potters. The relevant classification varies but in Pigot's time it was usually only 'Potters'.

1822 Pigot. *Pigot and Co.'s London & Provincial New Commercial Directory for 1822–3* (Norton 35). Address dated 24 June 1822.

1824 Pigot. *Pigot & Co.'s New Commercial Directory for 1824* (Norton 37). Address not dated.

1830 Pigot. *Pigot and Co.'s National Commercial Directory . . . 1830* (Norton 53, Norton 54, Norton 55). Address not dated.

1842 Pigot. *Pigot and Co.'s Royal National and Commercial Directory and Topography . . . July* [*or September*] *1842* (Norton 73, Norton 74, Norton 76). Address dated July or September 1842. Several different editions exist, including at least one not listed by Norton.

1844 Pigot. *Pigot and Co.'s Royal National and Commercial Directory and Topography . . . June 1844* (Norton 78). Address dated June 1844. Two different editions exist, one not listed by Norton. The Gloucestershire section is only a reprint from 1842 Pigot (above).

John Reed
Bristol

John Reed is believed to have been the author of the Bristol section which appeared in the second volume of Peter Barfoot and John Wilkes' *Universal British Directory*. He published his *New Bristol Directory* in 1792, but it consists simply of offprint pages from

the main directory bound with a new title page and dedication. As such it is listed here but omitted from the list of potters. The directory is not classified.
1792 Reed. *The New Bristol Directory for the Year 1792* (Norton 254). Dedication not dated.

William Robson
London
William Robson was a publisher of London directories who branched out briefly to cover the Home Counties in 1838 and many other English counties from 1839. Bristol appears in two editions, neither of which are dated although Norton lists them as 1839 and 1840. As far as this survey is concerned the contents are identical. The relevant classifications are 'Potters' and 'Stone Warehouses'.
1839 Robson. *Robson's Commercial Directory of London & the Nine Counties, viz. Beds, Cambridge, Gloster, Hunts, Norfolk, Suffolk, Wilts, and Parts of Berks and Bucks, with the City of Bristol, and Islands of Guernsey and Jersey . . . in Two Volumes . . . Vol. II containing Country Directory* (Norton 101). Not dated on title page of Volume 2.
1840 Robson. *Robson's Commercial Directory of London and the Western Counties, viz. Berks, Cornwall, Devon, Gloster, Hants, Somerset, and Wilts, with the Islands of Guernsey and Jersey — in Two Volumes . . . Vol. II containing Directory of the Counties* (Norton 105). Title page not dated. The Bristol section is purely a reprint from 1839 Robson (above), with four additional pages which are not relevant to this work.

W. Scammell & Co.
Bristol
W. Scammell & Co. published three directories in 1852 and 1853, all including Bristol. The Bristol information was the same in the two 1852 editions, but was updated for 1853. The relevant classification is 'Potters — Stone Ware'.
1852 Scammell. *Scammell & Co.'s City of Bristol and South Wales Directory . . . February 1852* (Norton 317, Shaw & Tipper 32). Address dated February 1852. Also *Scammell & Co.'s Gloucester, Bristol and South Wales Directory for 1853* (Norton 353). Address dated September 1852.
1853 Scammell. *Scammell & Co.'s Bristol General Directory . . . January 1853* (Norton 318, Shaw & Tipper 463). Address not dated.

Sharp & Co.
Bristol
Sharp & Co. published four directories of Bristol between 1903 and 1906, the first three titled *The New Bristol Directory*. The catalogue in the Bristol library lists directories of the same title published by G. du Boistel & Co., not listed by Shaw & Tipper, which may be the same, but their copies could not be located. As a result the 1903 and 1905 editions were not available for this survey. The relevant classifications are 'Bottle Manufacturers', 'Potters', 'Stone Jar and Bottle Manufacturers', and 'Stone Ware Manufacturers and Dealers'.
1903 Sharp. *The New Bristol Directory . . . 1903* (Shaw & Tipper 489). No copy available.
1904 Sharp. *The New Bristol Directory . . . 1904* (Shaw & Tipper 489). Preface not dated.
1905 Sharp. *The New Bristol Directory . . . 1905* (Shaw & Tipper 489). No copy available.
1906 Sharp. *Sharp's Bristol Directory, incorporating The New Bristol Directory . . . 1906* (Not listed by Shaw & Tipper). Preface not dated.

James Sketchley
Bristol
James Sketchley holds the distinction of publishing the first provincial directories

(of Birmingham) starting in 1763 and went on to issue the first directory of Bristol, which was then his home city, in 1775. The directory is not dated but Norton gives 1775 derived from the name of the mayor. The directory is not classified.
1775 Sketchley. *Sketchley's Bristol Directory* (Norton 251). Preface not dated.

Isaac Slater
Manchester and London

Isaac Slater succeeded James Pigot & Co. (qv) when Pigot died in 1843 and continued to produce similar directories until absorbed by Kelly's in 1892. Pigot's 1844 editions were actually published by Slater but the first edition to appear in his name was in 1846. Bristol was included in Gloucestershire surveys of 1850, 1858, 1868, and 1880, and was also listed as a city in its own right in directories of 1846 and 1857. As with the earlier Pigot issues, several different editions of each directory were produced, usually with different combinations of counties, and these can be confusing. Once again, all known editions are listed but those which are simply reprints are noted as such and excluded from the list of potters. The relevant classification varies but in Slater's time was either 'Potters' or, from 1850, 'Earthenware Manufacturers'.

1846 Slater. *Slater's National Commercial Directory of Ireland: Including Alphabetical Directories of Dublin, Belfast, Cork and Limerick, to which are added Classified Directories of the Important English Towns of Manchester, Liverpool, Birmingham, West Bromwich, Leeds, Sheffield and Bristol; and in Scotland, those of Glasgow, Paisley and Greenock . . . 1846* (Norton 81). Address dated March 1846. Also *Slater's National Commercial Directory of Ireland: Including Alphabetical Directories of Dublin, Belfast, Cork and Limerick, to which are added Classified Directories of the Isle of Man; Important English Towns of Manchester, Liverpool, Birmingham, West Bromwich, Leeds, Sheffield and Bristol; and in Scotland, those of Glasgow, Paisley and Greenock . . . 1846* (Norton 81a). Address dated September 1846. Also *Slater's Commercial Directory of the Isle on Man, and the Following Important English Towns — Manchester, Liverpool, Birmingham, West Bromwich, Leeds, Sheffield and Bristol; and in Scotland, those of Glasgow, Paisley and Greenock . . . 1846* (Norton 81b). No Address in the only copy located.

1847 Slater. *Slater's Classified Directories of the Following Important English Towns, Birmingham, Bristol, Derby, Leeds, Leicester, Liverpool, Manchester, Nottingham, Sheffield, and West Bromwich. In Scotland, Glasgow, Paisley, Johnstone and Greenock; together with the Isle of Man . . . 1847* (Related to Norton 82). The Bristol section is only a reprint from 1846 Slater (above).

1850 Slater. *Slater's (late Pigot & Co.) Royal National and Commercial Directory and Topography . . . 1850* (Norton 87, Norton 88, Norton 89, Shaw & Tipper 27, Shaw & Tipper 29). Address dated 1850 or January 1850.

1851 Slater. *Slater's (late Pigot & Co.) Royal National and Commercial Directory and Topography . . . 1851* (Norton 91, Shaw & Tipper 30). Address dated 1851. The Gloucestershire section is only a reprint from 1850 Slater (above).

1852 Slater. *Slater's (late Pigot & Co.) Royal National and Commercial Directory and Topography . . . 1852–3* (Norton 97, Shaw & Tipper 34). Address dated December 1852. The Gloucestershire section is only a reprint from 1850 Slater (above).

1857 Slater. *Slater's (late Pigot & Co.'s) Royal National Commercial Directory of the Important Towns of Manchester, Birmingham, Bristol, Glasgow, Paisley, Greenock, Johnstone and Port Glasgow, together with a Commercial, Topographical and General Directory of Ireland . . . 1857* (Related to Shaw & Tipper 162). Address dated 1857.

1858 Slater. *Slater's (late Pigot & Co.) Royal National and Commercial Directory and Topography . . . 1858–9* (Shaw & Tipper 39). Address dated December 1858.

1859 Slater. *Slater's (late Pigot & Co.) Royal National and Commercial Directory and Topography . . . 1859* (Shaw & Tipper 29). The Gloucestershire section is only a reprint from 1858 Slater (above).

1868 Slater. *Slater's (late Pigot & Co.) Royal National Commercial Directory and Topography . . . 1868* (Shaw & Tipper 29). Address dated January 1868.
1880 Slater. *Slater's Royal National Commercial Directory . . . 1880* (Shaw & Tipper 1694). Address not dated.

Town & County Directories Ltd.
Edinburgh and Manchester

The firm of Town & County Directories Ltd. published their first directory in 1898, and built up an extensive business producing trades directories covering many districts in England, Wales and Scotland, which continued until at least 1950. Amongst their first publications were five annual directories of Bristol, dating between 1899 and 1903–4, which are not listed by Shaw & Tipper. Thereafter Bristol was not covered again until 1921. The relevant classifications are 'Potters' and (in 1903 only) 'Stone Bottle and Jar Manufacturers'.
1899 Town. *Bristol and District Trades' Directory . . . 1899* (Not listed by Shaw & Tipper). No preface.
1900 Town. *Bristol and District Trades' Directory . . . 1900* (Not listed by Shaw & Tipper). No preface.
1901 Town. *Bristol and District Trades' Directory . . . 1901* (Not listed by Shaw & Tipper). No preface.
1902 Town. *Bristol and District Trades' Directory . . . 1902–3* (Not listed by Shaw & Tipper). No preface.
1903 Town. *Bristol and District Trades' Directory . . . 1903–4* (Not listed by Shaw & Tipper). No preface.

William Tunnicliff
Bath

William Tunnicliff described himself as a land surveyor and published a Topographical Survey of Staffordshire, Cheshire and Lancashire in 1787. The book was expanded with the addition of Somerset, Gloucestershire and Worcestershire for an edition dated 1789, with the original pages simply reprinted. The Gloucestershire section includes a list of principal merchants and manufacturers with a short non-classified section for Bristol in which only one potter appears.
1789 Tunnicliff. *A Topographical Survey of the Counties of Somerset, Gloucester, Worcester, Stafford, Chester, and Lancaster . . . 1789* (Norton 7). Dedication dated December 1788.

Thomas Underhill
See: William Holden

Universal
See: Peter Barfoot & John Wilkes

Webster & Co.
London

Webster & Co.'s main publication was the *Royal Red Book or Court and Fashionable Register*, issued from 1852 to 1939, but they branched out to produce a directory of Bristol with Glamorgan and Monmouthshire in 1865 and a directory of Reading in 1874. Their 1865 directory appears to have been either pirated or reprinted by arrangement in 1966 by J.G. Harrod & Co. (qv), who operated from neighbouring premises in London. The relevant classifications are 'Earthenware Manufacturers' and 'Stoneware Manufacturers'.

1865 Webster. *Webster & Co.'s Postal and Commercial Directory of the City of Bristol, and Counties of Glamorgan & Monmouth . . . 1865* (Shaw & Tipper 44). Preface dated October 1865.

J. Wright & Co.

Bristol

J. Wright & Co. took over the annual Bristol directory from the Mathews family in 1870. They remodelled it somewhat and published it annually until 1903 although the Mathews name was retained until 1880. From 1904 through to 1923 the directory was still issued with the Wright name although it was published by Kelly's Directories Ltd. Thereafter it appeared under Kelly's own name. The Kelly's editions of 1904 to 1906 are included in this section for completeness. The relevant classifications are 'Potters', 'Stone Ware Dealers' (1870 only), 'Stone Ware Manufacturers and Dealers' (1871–1893), and 'Stone Jar & Bottle Manufacturers' (from 1894).

1870 Wright. *Mathews's Bristol Directory, with Adjacent Villages, remodelled by J. Wright & Co. . . . 1870* (Shaw & Tipper 474). Preface dated 25 February 1870.

1871 Wright. *Mathews's Bristol Directory, with Adjacent Villages, remodelled by J. Wright & Co. . . . 1871* (Shaw & Tipper 474). Preface dated 2 January 1871.

1872 Wright. *Mathews's Bristol Directory, with Adjacent Villages, remodelled by J. Wright & Co. . . . 1872* (Shaw & Tipper 474). Preface dated 26 January 1872.

1873 Wright. *Mathews's Bristol Directory, with Adjacent Villages, remodelled by J. Wright & Co. . . . 1873* (Shaw & Tipper 474). Preface dated 18 January 1872 (sic).

1874 Wright. *Mathews's Bristol Directory, with Adjacent Villages, remodelled by J. Wright & Co. . . . 1874* (Shaw & Tipper 474). Preface dated 16 December 1873.

1875 Wright. *Mathews's Bristol Directory, with Adjacent Villages, remodelled by J. Wright & Co. . . . 1875* (Shaw & Tipper 474). Preface dated 19 December 1874.

1876 Wright. *Mathews's Bristol Directory, with Adjacent Villages, remodelled by J. Wright & Co. . . . 1876* (Shaw & Tipper 474). Preface dated 11 December 1876 (sic).

1877 Wright. *Mathews's Bristol Directory, with Adjacent Villages, remodelled by J. Wright & Co. . . . 1877* (Shaw & Tipper 474). Preface dated 13 December 1876

1878 Wright. *Mathews's Bristol Directory, with Adjacent Villages, remodelled by J. Wright & Co. . . . 1878* (Shaw & Tipper 474). Preface dated 15 December 1877.

1879 Wright. *Mathews's Bristol Directory, with Adjacent Villages, remodelled by J. Wright & Co. . . . 1879* (Shaw & Tipper 474). Preface dated 30 December 1878.

1880 Wright. *J. Wright & Co.'s (Mathews') Bristol & Clifton Directory, with nearly a hundred adjacent Villages . . . 1880* (Shaw & Tipper 478). Preface dated 15 December (no year).

1881 Wright. *J. Wright & Co.'s (Mathews') Bristol & Clifton Directory, with nearly a hundred adjacent Villages . . . 1881* (Shaw & Tipper 478). Preface dated December 1880.

1882 Wright. *J. Wright & Co.'s (Mathews') Bristol & Clifton Directory, with nearly a hundred adjacent Villages . . . 1882* (Shaw & Tipper 478). Preface dated December 1881.

1883 Wright. *J. Wright & Co.'s (Mathews') Bristol & Clifton Directory, with nearly a hundred adjacent Villages . . . 1883* (Shaw & Tipper 478). Preface dated December 1882.

1884 Wright. *J. Wright & Co.'s (Mathews') Bristol & Clifton Directory, with nearly a hundred adjacent Villages . . . 1884* (Shaw & Tipper 478). Preface dated December 1883.

1885 Wright. *J. Wright & Co.'s (Mathews') Bristol & Clifton Directory, with nearly a hundred adjacent Villages . . . 1885* (Shaw & Tipper 478). Preface dated December 1884.

1886 Wright. *J. Wright & Co.'s (Mathews') Bristol & Clifton Directory, with nearly a hundred adjacent Villages . . . 1886* (Shaw & Tipper 478). Preface dated December 1885.

1887 Wright. *J. Wright & Co.'s (Mathews') Bristol & Clifton Directory, with upwards of a hundred and thirty adjacent Villages . . . 1887* (Shaw & Tipper 478). Preface dated December 1886.

1888 Wright. *J. Wright & Co.'s (Mathews') Bristol & Clifton Directory, with upwards of a hundred*

and fifty adjacent Villages . . . 1888 (Shaw & Tipper 478). Preface dated December 1887.
1889 Wright. *J. Wright & Co.'s (Mathews') Bristol & Clifton Directory, with upwards of a hundred and fifty adjacent Villages . . . 1889* (Shaw & Tipper 478). Preface dated December 1888.
1890 Wright. *J. Wright & Co.'s (Mathews') Bristol & Clifton Directory, with upwards of a hundred and fifty adjacent Villages . . . 1890* (Shaw & Tipper 478). Preface dated December 1889.
1891 Wright. *J. Wright & Co.'s (Mathews') Bristol & Clifton Directory, with upwards of a hundred and fifty adjacent Villages . . . 1891* (Shaw & Tipper 478). Preface dated December 1890.
1892 Wright. *J. Wright & Co.'s (Mathews') Bristol & Clifton Directory, with upwards of a hundred and fifty adjacent Villages . . . 1892* (Shaw & Tipper 478). Preface dated December 1891.
1893 Wright. *J. Wright & Co.'s (Mathews') Bristol and Clifton Directory, with upwards of a hundred and fifty adjacent Villages . . . 1893* (Shaw & Tipper 478). Preface dated December 1892.
1894 Wright. *J. Wright & Co.'s (Mathews') Bristol and Clifton Directory, with upwards of a hundred and fifty adjacent Villages . . . 1894* (Shaw & Tipper 478). Preface dated 12 December 1893.
1895 Wright. *J. Wright & Co.'s (Mathews') Bristol and Clifton Directory, with upwards of a hundred and fifty adjacent Villages . . . 1895* (Shaw & Tipper 478). Preface dated December 1894.
1896 Wright. *J. Wright & Co.'s (Mathews') Bristol and Clifton Directory, with upwards of a hundred and fifty adjacent Villages . . . 1896* (Shaw & Tipper 478). Preface dated December 1895.
1897 Wright. *J. Wright & Co.'s (Mathews') Bristol and Clifton Directory, with upwards of a hundred and fifty adjacent Villages . . . 1897* (Shaw & Tipper 478). Preface dated December 1896.
1898 Wright. *J. Wright & Co.'s (Mathews') Bristol and Clifton Directory, with a hundred and fifty-three adjacent Villages . . . 1898* (Shaw & Tipper 478). Preface dated December 1897.
1899 Wright. *J. Wright & Co.'s (Mathews') Bristol and Clifton Directory, with a hundred and fifty-five adjacent Villages . . . 1899* (Shaw & Tipper 478). Preface dated December 1898.
1900 Wright. *J. Wright & Co.'s (Mathews') Bristol and Clifton Directory, with a hundred and fifty-five adjacent Villages . . . 1900* (Shaw & Tipper 478). Preface dated December 1899.
1901 Wright. *J. Wright & Co.'s (Mathews') Bristol and Clifton Directory, with a hundred and fifty-five adjacent Villages . . . 1901* (Shaw & Tipper 478). Preface dated December 1900.
1902 Wright. *J. Wright & Co.'s (Mathews') Bristol and Clifton Directory, with a hundred and fifty-five adjacent Villages . . . 1902* (Shaw & Tipper 478). Preface dated December 1901.
1903 Wright. *J. Wright & Co.'s (Mathews') Bristol and Clifton Directory, with a hundred and fifty-five adjacent Villages . . . 1903* (Shaw & Tipper 478). Preface dated December 1902.
1904 Wright. *J. Wright & Co.'s Bristol Directory, with adjacent Villages . . . 1904* (Shaw & Tipper 478). Preface not dated.
1905 Wright. *Wright's Bristol Directory, including Westbury-on-Trym, Shirehampton, Horfield and part of Henbury, with the adjacent Villages . . . 1905* (Shaw & Tipper 478). Preface not dated.
1906 Wright. *Wright's Bristol Directory, including Westbury-on-Trym, Shirehampton, Horfield and part of Henbury . . . 1906* (Shaw & Tipper 478). Preface dated December 1905.

Other Publishers

Several directories by other publishers have been examined but found not to be relevant to this survey. They are listed below for completeness:

The Gloucestershire Directory . . . 1820 (Norton 248). By R. Gell & T. Bradshaw, Gloucester. This directory does not include Bristol.

Mercer & Crocker's General, Topographical and Historical Directory for the Counties of Monmouthshire, Herefordshire, Gloucestershire . . . 1871 (Shaw & Tipper 54). This directory does not include Bristol.

Mercer & Crocker's General, Topographical, and Historical Directory for Monmouthshire, Herefordshire, Gloucestershire, &c. . . . 1875 (Shaw & Tipper 54). Another Mercer & Crocker directory which does not include Bristol.

Mercer & Crocker's General, Topographical, and Historical Directory for the Counties of Monmouthshire, Herefordshire, Gloucestershire and . . . places in Glamorganshire and Radnorshire . . . 1876 (Shaw & Tipper 54). Another Mercer & Crocker directory which does not include Bristol.

Deacon's Court Guide, Gazetteer and Royal Blue-Book: a Fashionable Register and General Survey of the County of Gloucester . . . 1880 (Shaw & Tipper 456). This directory includes Bristol but does not cover commercial firms.
Deacon's Court Guide, Gazetteer and Royal Blue-Book . . . of the Western Division of Gloucestershire, Chippenham, Devizes, Frome, Marlborough, Shepton Mallet, Bristol [etc.] . . . 1882 (Shaw & Tipper 169). Another Deacon directory which includes Bristol but does not cover commercial firms.
The Gloucester Court Guide and County Blue-Book . . . 1899 (Shaw & Tipper 456). Another Deacon directory which includes Bristol but does not cover commercial firms.
Bale's Trades Directory . . . [of Gloucs., Somerset, Wilts., Dorset] . . . 1900 (Shaw & Tipper 75). This directory does not include Bristol.

Bibliography

Bristol Potteries

Britton, Frank, *English Delftware in the Bristol Collection*. Sotheby Publications, London, 1982.

Jackson, Reg & Philomena, and Price, Roger, 'Bristol Potters and Potteries 1600–1800', *Journal of Ceramic History*, No. 12, 1982.

Levitt, Sarah, *Pountneys — The Bristol Pottery at Fishponds 1905–1969*. Redcliffe Press Ltd., Bristol, 1990.

Owen, Hugh, *Two Centuries of Ceramic Art in Bristol, being a History of the Manufacture of 'The True Porcelain' by Richard Champion . . . with an Account of the Delft, Earthenware and Enamel Glass Works from Original Sources*. Printed privately for the author by John Bellows, Gloucester, 1873.

Pountney, W.J., *Old Bristol Potteries, being an Account of the Old Potters and Potteries of Bristol and Brislington, between 1650 and 1850, with some pages on the old Chapel of St. Anne, Brislington*. J.W. Arrowsmith Ltd., Bristol, 1920 (reprinted by E.P. Publishing Ltd., Wakefield, 1972).

Thomas, Nicholas, and Wilson, Arnold, *Ceramics in Bristol — The Fine Wares 1670–1970*. Catalogue of an Exhibition held at the City of Bristol Museum and Art Gallery, September 1979 to January 1980.

Witt, Cleo, 'Good Cream Color Ware — The Bristol Pottery 1786–1968', *The Connoisseur*, Vol. 202, No. 811, September 1979.

General

Cushion, John P., *Handbook of Pottery and Porcelain Marks*. Faber & Faber, London, 1956 (fourth revised edition 1980).

Godden, Geoffrey A., *Encyclopaedia of British Pottery and Porcelain Marks*. Herbert Jenkins, London, 1964.

Jewitt, Llewellynn, *The Ceramic Art of Great Britain*. Virtue & Co., London, 1878 (second revised edition 1883, reprinted by Paul P.B. Minet, Chicheley, 1971).

Directories

Norton, Jane, *Guide to the National and Provincial Directories of England and Wales, Excluding London, Published Before 1856*. Royal Historical Society, London, 1950 (reprinted with corrections, 1984).

Shaw, Gareth, and Tipper, Allison, *British Directories: A Bibliography and Guide to Directories Published in England and Wales (1850–1950) and Scotland (1773–1950)*. Leicester University Press, Leicester, 1989.